Did you see Us?

PERCEPTIONS ON TRUTH AND RECONCILIATION

ISSN 2371-347X

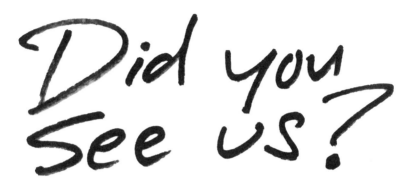

REUNION, REMEMBRANCE, AND RECLAMATION

at an Urban Indian Residential School

SURVIVORS OF
THE ASSINIBOIA INDIAN RESIDENTIAL SCHOOL

UNIVERSITY OF
MANITOBA PRESS

Did You See Us?: Reunion, Remembrance, and Reclamation at an Urban
Indian Residential School
© Assiniboia Residential School Legacy Group 2021

25   24 23   22   21   1   2   3   4   5

University of Manitoba Press
Winnipeg, Manitoba, Canada
Treaty 1 Territory
uofmpress.ca

Cataloguing data available from Library and Archives Canada
Perceptions on Truth and Reconciliation, ISSN 2371-347X ; 5
ISBN 978-0-88755-907-5 (PAPER)
ISBN 978-0-88755-924-2 (PDF)
ISBN 978-0-88755-920-4 (EPUB)
ISBN 978-0-88755-925-9 (BOUND)

Cover and interior design by Vincent Design

"Residential School in City's Backyard," by Catherine
Mitchell, is reprinted with permission of *Winnipeg Free Press*.

Printed in Canada

This book has been published with the help of a grant from the
Federation for the Humanities and Social Sciences, through the Awards
to Scholarly Publications Program, using funds provided by the
Social Sciences and Humanities Research Council of Canada.

The University of Manitoba Press acknowledges the financial support for
its publication program provided by the Government of Canada through
the Canada Book Fund, the Canada Council for the Arts, the Manitoba
Department of Sport, Culture, and Heritage, the Manitoba Arts Council,
and the Manitoba Book Publishing Tax Credit.

Funded by the Government of Canada   Canadä

LAND ACKNOWLEDGEMENT

We acknowledge we are on First Nations land, Turtle Island, inhabited by First Nations from time immemorial.

For thousands of years, First Nations people—the Anishinaabe, Cree, Dakota, Dene, and Anishininew Nations—walked and lived on this land and knew it to be the centre of their lives and spirituality.

The Anishinaabe call this land Manitou Ahbee, the place where the Creator resides.

We acknowledge this became the homeland of the Métis people.

We acknowledge and welcome the many people from countries all over the world who have come to join us, Turtle Island's First Nations, in calling this land our home.

We acknowledge we are now all bound together by Treaty 1.

—Theodore Fontaine

CONTENTS

PART VI: THE CITY OF WINNIPEG REMEMBERS

PART VII: REUNION, REMEMBRANCE, AND RECLAMATION

ILLUSTRATIONS

DEDICATION

Survivors of the Assiniboia Indian Residential School have shared powerful remembrances at our reunions and meetings and through the compilation of our stories in this commemorative book.

It is important to understand the meaning of the word "story." In English, a story must be clarified as to whether it's fictional or non-fictional. There isn't that distinction in the Anishinaabe language. You speak as if you were holding an eagle feather or had your hand on the Bible. Your word is your word and your story is truth. I would like to acknowledge and attribute this teaching to Roger Roulette, a renowned expert in the Ojibwe language.

Children from more than eighty First Nations and other Indigenous communities attended Assiniboia. The first students came from First Nations in Manitoba. Slowly, students from Alberta, Saskatchewan, Ontario, and Quebec became part of the Assiniboia community. Those who survived genocide and violence while incarcerated in their first Indian residential schools became leaders in the evolution of the Indian residential schools system. Transition to life at Assiniboia brought us into a comfortable and safe urban environment. We are grateful to Reverend Father Omer Robidoux, Assiniboia's principal, whose grace and leadership brought us individually and collectively to a better place.

This evolution is a testament to the adaptability of Indian children to survive colonization policies put into practice by governments, churches, and Indian residential school administrators. Yet approximately 60 to 70 percent of the former 600 students of Assiniboia departed this earth early. We miss them, and now, in our private moments, we relive the stories of the joy, love, and friendship we shared with those now departed from our realm.

We remember all of our departed schoolmates, too numerous to list, but never forgotten. We remember the first graduates of Assiniboia, Oliver Nelson and Joe Guy Wood, and the many who followed through different eras, including wonderful singer and performer

Percy Tuesday; smooth skater Joe Malcolm; gracious Alma Patrick; the Burns sisters from KeeSee; storyteller Dennis Fontaine and all those from Sagkeeng; the Wood and Harper clans from the Island Lake area; the Nepinaks of Pine Creek; and our friends from Norway House, God's Lake, God's River, Cross Lake, Deer Lake, Roseau River, Eagle Lake, Couchiching, Sandy Lake, and many other communities.

Those who are gone have left their presence in our hearts. Their footsteps are indelible impressions in the grassy playing fields and on the wooden floors of our classrooms building. We hold their memories sacred. They are with us when we are on the grounds of Assiniboia, their spirits ever-present in our lives.

This book is dedicated to each and every one of them, our beloved brothers and sisters.

— Theodore Fontaine

PREFACE

Theodore Fontaine

As a prelude to the historical context of remembering the Assiniboia Indian Residential School, we must recall the events and reasons leading up to the establishment of an Indian residential school in a large metropolis like Winnipeg.

This history reveals the impacts experienced by children, families, parents, and grandparents of both the colonizers and the colonized. It must be a continuing narrative for history's sake. This is not the beginning story nor an ending story, but a true depiction of a central part of a history now embedded in the collective library of knowledge of the survival of the First Peoples of Canada.

Although much has been written about the history of Canada and the relationship of governments and settlers with the First Peoples of Canada, testimony of this true history as lived by the First Peoples of Canada has been brief.

As former students, now adults, we are Survivors of the infamous Indian residential schools system. Our testimony, shared at our reunions, is shared here as remembrances and reclamation of our lived experiences.

Yet the history of the Assiniboia Indian Residential School has been an enigma, a unique story left untold. Its existence and operation, from 1958 to 1973, were almost unknown to residents of the City of Winnipeg, including those living in River Heights, the neighbourhood where this Indian school was situated. What story was never told? Did you see us?

The history of Assiniboia includes close to 1,000 individual stories, the lived experiences of former students, staff, parents, River Heights residents, and many others in the First Nations and non-Indigenous communities of Winnipeg and Manitoba. This book offers a small selection of these stories. More are left to be told.

The Survivors of Assiniboia have deliberately included the word "Indian" in this book, to describe not only a school, but more importantly, the intent of an Indian school: to make Indian children ashamed of who we were, and to force us to abandon our First Nations identity. We sanitize or minimize the reality of what an Indian residential school was when the word "Indian" is avoided in an effort to evoke an acceptable concept of residential schools, also known as boarding schools, usually reserved for the elite in society.

Through relentless efforts to assimilate the original people of this land, we have at various times been called Indians, Natives, half-breeds, Métis, Aboriginal, Indigenous, and First Nations. Society is generally more comfortable with words that try to erase the derogatory connotations of terminology used in the heyday of colonization, including "Indian."

To be clear, our identities arise from thousands of years of nation building, from which our birthright is to proudly self-identify in this region as Anishinaabe, Cree, Dakota, Dene, or Anishininew. Across Turtle Island, there are countless First Nations, each with its distinct identity, history, and heritage.

The transfer of Indian children from different Indian residential schools on Manitoba Indian reserves was part of an overall plan by the Government of Canada to implement a further step in the ongoing attempt to assimilate Indians. The institutionalization of Indian children, begun in 1831, was formalized in 1920 by Canada's Parliament with the legislated mandatory removal of children from their families. These children were locked up in Indian residential schools operating across Canada.

The Indian residential school policy and era were not intended to support or educate our people, but to get us out of the way of settler development and access to the wealth of Canada's natural resources. Implementation of the policy, primarily carried out by churches acting for the Canadian government, aimed to displace our Nations, destroy our traditional ways of life, our customs, cultural and linguistic heritage, legal rights, spirituality, and governmental and societal structures, and the very identities of the Indigenous Peoples of Canada. Canada's residential schools policy targeted children to ensure continuous destruction of our First Nations identity from one generation to the next.

Assiniboia was the first Indian residential school to provide high-school education in a major urban environment in Manitoba. Each of us had attended Indian residential schools from about the ages of six or seven, with schools situated both on Indian reserves and in rural and northern Manitoba communities. At first we thought that being transferred to Assiniboia was just another step in the progression of our incarceration. Yet, the Assiniboia Indian Residential School, by design or inadvertently, was a place where students began to peek out of a dark place and realize that we could live amongst the colonizers and attain some measure of adaptation to our changed lives.

Our stories began to weave together at Assiniboia. Now a little older, and having been away from our families and homes for so many years already, we began to emerge as friends and something like family. Our new reality included some freedoms and some amenities. With plenty of good food to eat, we began to reclaim our individual identities and to emerge as young First Nations adults. We began to find our voices, our laughter, and to value our relationships.

We were slowly introduced to a larger urban society and its amenities, including social, arts, and sports events. Within a few years, these new realities were further enhanced and we began to experience some freedom from the perils and trauma of incarceration in our previous residential school captivity.

As Assiniboia progressed over the years, students did not have to be at the facility full-time. Assiniboia slowly transformed into a hostel, with older Indian youth transferred in from residential schools in other provinces. Given nutritious lunch bags, they began to be bussed to various high schools around the city, including those within the River Heights community.

Many Assiniboia students went on to higher education, often later in life. Those from the earliest years wished that the positive adaptations to life at Assiniboia had been their experience. Sadly, many were so damaged by their early childhood incarceration that their lives were lost early in adulthood.

Assiniboia was an unprecedented success in providing a sensible and successful model, accomplishing to some extent the government's policy of assimilation by influencing the transition of Indian youth to urban living and white societal "norms." Yet, even then, and throughout our lives, we never gave up our First Nations heritage and identity. Most of us have worked hard to reclaim our identity, culture, language, family, and community.

The legacy of Assiniboia is the blending of stories not only of Survivors, but also of many in the community. This includes the residents of River Heights, who lived along the same roads and streets as Assiniboia with their children, yet didn't know who we were or why we were there.

Attending our 2017 reunion, we experienced a community outpouring of sorrow and regret that they had never been told about us or invited to engage with us. Those feelings were woven into their desire to get to know us now and to welcome us into their community.

There are the stories of the priests, nuns, teachers, and staff of Assiniboia, who despite the miserly funding of the federal government, treated us with kindness and respect, sincerely working to give us a good chance to trust, adapt, and to heal. They tried to make sure our learning included literature, art, music, sports, and the right to make choices and decisions for ourselves.

There are also the stories of youth in the community who went to other high schools with us, who competed with us in sports events, even some who tried to humiliate us for being Indian. There are stories of some who befriended us without racism, discrimination, or stereotyping. Some became lifelong friends, some we married.

The real legacy of Assiniboia is a true experience of reunion, reconciliation, and reclamation, hard-earned by students and community alike, reconciliation that came about many years after Assiniboia closed in 1973. The seeds were sown as early as opening day in September 1958, when the first class of students was welcomed off the buses that transferred them from the hellish experience of previous Indian residential schools. From that moment, we all slowly emerged into who we really were, led by a little beam of light shining on us, held up by Principal Father Robidoux.

Since 2013, a small group of us have banded together to share our experiences, to catch up on each other's lives, to reminisce about the precious, loving years when we were children before residential schools, and the difficult years after. It is a monthly reunion for those of us who now get together to push forward our collective vision to preserve the history and legacy of the Assiniboia Indian Residential School.

Many relationships that took hold among Assiniboia students have lasted through our lifetimes, dating back to the first-year class from 1958–59. More than fifty years later, in 2015 some of us got together in an impromptu reunion. We came together on the grounds of the Assiniboia school where we had experienced joyous freedom on the skating rinks, baseball diamonds, and open green playing fields. We huddled in a tipi in a driving rain all day, swapping stories and remembrances, that rain awakening a desire to join hands and hearts once again. The Creator embedded our resolve and this became the turning point, the recognition of our need to reclaim our own voices and our history, and an opportunity to make sure our story was heard. From this sodden beginning was born the intention to never let our Assiniboia experience disappear from the annals of history.

Some of us got together again in January 2016 to continue the conversation. We began working with Andrew Woolford, professor of sociology and criminology at the University of Manitoba and former president of the International Association of Genocide Scholars. We knew that Andrew's expertise in genocide studies specifically concerns the destruction of Indigenous Peoples in North America. Our collaboration is a perfect synergy of his research interests and our determination to never let our experiences be forgotten.

Regular meetings since then have resulted in the creation of a community-based research project and the establishment of the

Assiniboia Indian Residential School Legacy Group, an incorporated non-profit organization. Over time, we set three main goals: to organize a reunion for former students, to design and seek funding for a commemorative marker to be built on the former school site, and to create an educational book about Assiniboia. Together, we are reclaiming our former school and its legacy.

Did You See Us? is the book that tells our story. Our individual remembrances were recorded live at a 2017 reunion, transcribed, and then reworked or authored by each former student, creating our own chapters. Our stories are told by era, beginning with the first students at Assiniboia, from 1958 to 1959, when it was fully a residential school. Students from that era lived there for ten months of the year, attending classes and chapel, sleeping in large dormitories, eating together, and escaping to our precious outdoor field, then bordered by high fencing. The chapters proceed through the years to the last students, who hostelled at Assiniboia while attending other high schools in Winnipeg.

The students of each era of the school experienced it differently, and we wanted the book to allow these differences to gather side-by-side, just as Survivors from the different eras gathered side-by-side at the school reunion. Community residents as well have their own stories to tell, as do journalists and the City of Winnipeg historical buildings officer.

The Canadian Centre for Child Protection has been an advocate and strong supporter, welcoming us into Assiniboia's former classrooms building, where the Centre passionately defends Canadian children. Centre officials hosted our reunions on the grounds of the Assiniboia school, opened the building to us, and continue to encourage our visits and remembrances. A photograph of the 1958–59 first-year class is mounted within, a remembrance that the protection of Indian children is a long-standing legacy of the very building itself.

This book honours all who are part of the collective story of Assiniboia. Each has contributed to community reconciliation in a sustained and meaningful way. Like the Assiniboine River that flows just beyond our playing fields, our stories run together, sometimes slowly, sometimes in a torrent. They rise and fall with memories and emotions. There is no beginning and there is no end, there is only the ebb and flow of the years gone by and the story that flows forward to future generations.

In consultation and collaboration with many community supporters, we continue to work toward permanent remembrance of Assiniboia to commemorate the turning point it played not only in our lives but in the community of Winnipeg. This commemorative book, recognition of the former school site, and reclamation of a permanent gathering place on the playing fields will be elements of the legacy we leave behind. We trust that those who come after us will hold our past tenderly in their hearts and understand at what cost did we come here.

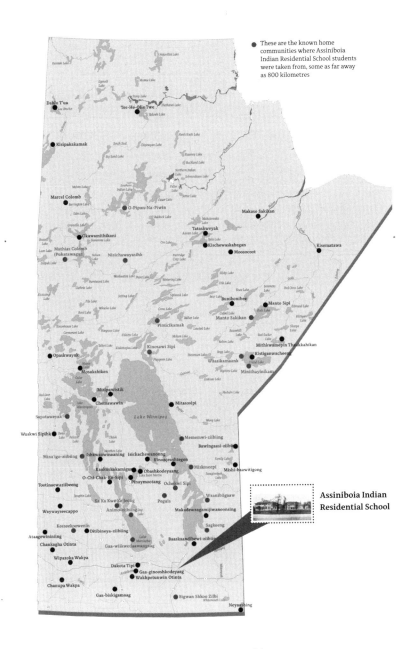

These are the known home communities where Assiniboia Indian Residential School students were taken from, some as far away as 800 kilometres

Dahlu T'ua
Tes-He-Olie Twe
Kisipakakamak
Marcel Colomb
O-Pipon-Na-Piwin
Makaso Sakikan
Okawamithikani
Tataskweyak
Mathias Colomb (Pukatawagan)
Nisichawayasihk
Kischewaskahegan
Moosocoot
Kisematawa
Bunibonibee
Manto Sipi
Manto Sakikan
Pimicikamak
Mithkwamepin Theakkahikan
Kinosawi Sipi
Kistiganwacheeng
Opaskwayak
Waasikamaank
Minithayinikam
Mosakahiken
Misipawistik
Chemawawin
Mitasosipi
Lake Winnipeg
Sapotaweyak
Mememwi-ziibiing
Wuskwi Sipihk
Bawingaasi-ziibii
Mina'igo-ziibiing
Ishkwaawinaaning
Isickachewanoong
Kinonjeoshtegon
Miskoseepi
Mishi-baawitigong
Kasihtiskakamigan
Obashkodeyaang
O-Chi-Chak-Ko-Sipi
Pinaymootang
Ochekwi Sipi
Tootinaowaziibeeng
Waanibiigaaw
Ka Ka Kwe Ke Jeong
Animo-ziibiing
Makadewaagamijiwanoonsing
Waywayseecappo
Peguis
Sagkeeng
Keeseekoowenin
Ditibineya-ziibiing
Ataagewininiing
Baaskaandibewi-ziibii
Chankagha Otinta
Gaa-wiikwedaawangaag
Wipazoka Wakpa
Dakota Tipi
Gaa-ginooshkodeyaang
Chanupa Wakpa
Wakhpetunwin Otinta
Gaa-biskigamaag
Bigwan Shkoo Zilbi
Neyaashiing

Assiniboia Indian Residential School

Map of student home communities.

PART I
THE RESIDENTIAL YEARS, 1958–67

Figure 1. Assiniboia Indian Residential School, c. 1950–70.

When the Survivor advisors for the project were approached about how the book should be organized, they were clear that remembrances should be presented in chronological order. Every year of students had their own distinct experience of Assiniboia, but the differences are most apparent between those who attended Assiniboia as a residential school and those who were hostelled there and ferried off to non-Indigenous high schools for their education. Each group faced their own challenges, and each found their own ways to survive and even thrive in their particular era.

The remembrances that follow begin with those of Survivors who were there when the school opened. They feature recollections of staff members and interactions with the settler community beyond the school. As the school enters the 1960s, remembrances turn toward sporting successes, student relationships, and, on occasion, a bit of mischief. In 1967, under a policy of integration, students are no longer educated within the Assiniboia classrooms building; instead, they attend Winnipeg high schools such as Kelvin, Grant Park, and Saint Mary's. Assiniboia provides us a unique opportunity, given its relatively short lifespan, to hear from Survivors from its opening until its close. The same is often not possible for Indian residential schools that operated from the late 1800s, or even early 1900s, into the late twentieth century.

3

WE ALL GOT ALONG
AND TREATED EACH OTHER WITH KINDNESS AND RESPECT

Dorothy-Ann Crate (née James)
Manto Sakikan – God's Lake First Nation, Manitoba[1]
Attended Assiniboia, 1958–62

In 1958–59, Assiniboia Indian Residential School on 621 Academy Road in Winnipeg was the first residential high school in the province of Manitoba.

Most of us students were transferred from Fort Alexander Indian Residential School, situated on the Sagkeeng First Nation along the Winnipeg River. That school provided classes only up to grade eight.

There were ninety-eight young girls and boys who started at Assiniboia Indian Residential School in the district of River Heights on the west side of Winnipeg, towards the Tuxedo Area.

The principal at Fort Alexander, Father Bilodeau, or any other administrative person, had never told us early in the year that we were going to be transferred to Winnipeg.

Students from Fort Alexander were not too anxious to move to Winnipeg, as most of them had their families living at the Fort Alexander Reserve (Sagkeeng). But for the students from northern Manitoba, we were overwhelmingly excited to get to know the huge city of Winnipeg. Of course, we really didn't know what to expect or the whereabouts of where our school was going to be situated. We got the news around the last long weekend in May 1958, after all the Fort Alexander students went home for a short long-weekend holiday. The remaining students from the northern communities usually stayed at school.

Father Bilodeau had a meeting with the remaining students, and this was the day that he told us about the new school that we were going to in the fall. He told us that we would take a trip to Winnipeg to go and see our new school.

We were driven to Winnipeg in a truck with no seats; we all had to sit on the floor. There were two little windows on each side of the closed truck, which was driven by one of the Religious Brothers. As we were travelling, I guess it was on Main Street, one of the girls yelled, "Look at that beer bottle!"—it was spinning around in the air. We all turned quickly to look out of the little windows, it looked so funny to us. Then one of the girls said, "I wonder if there is beer in it?" We all started laughing hard and loud. I think we sort of scared our driver. Anyways, that was our funny and exciting ride.

I guess we must have come all the way down Main Street and Portage Avenue to Academy Road, until we arrived where the new residential school was going to be.

Mind you, while we were there, a train came by and sure made a lot of noise and shook the building. We all said, "Oh my, that train is going to keep us awake." One of the girls said, "Oh well, that will be our wake-up bell, no more Sister's bell."

Figure 2. Portage and Main, 13 November 1958.

We pulled into the driveway and followed the driver to the building. I guess the principal came in a different car, but I cannot recall if anybody else came.

We toured around the stale, smelly building, and we were scaring each other at the same time, saying that we might find a dead body as we went to all the rooms.

We were glad that the building was cleaned up before we came back to school in the middle of August 1958.

Our recreation room was on the main floor on the west side of the school. Our washrooms were off the hallway on the main floor. There were washrooms and shower rooms upstairs, but we were never allowed to go upstairs during the day unless there was an emergency.

There were two huge dormitories for us upstairs, one on the west side and one on the south side, and the beds were arranged row by row.

The boys' side of the residential school was on the east side, overlooking the principal's office. The staff room was at the front of the building across from the office. From the windows of his office or the staff room, the principal could keep an eye on us all the time.

We, the girls, were never allowed to mingle with the boys, not even in the cafeteria, as there were designated sections for boys and girls. As each had their own side of the room, there was no such luck to sit with boys during our mealtimes. If we got caught with a love note, it was read aloud in the cafeteria during lunch hour, then it was "Wow!"

After, we were given our class schedules, school chores, and most of all our school rules. These were not too strict, as we were allowed to smoke at the designated time. We also had a canteen after classes. We were able to purchase our cigarettes, drinks, and candy bars at this time. I don't remember chips, except Cracker Jack and boxed popcorn.

Also, our in-school chores were designated for two weeks at a time, then we changed our work. It was nice, and we looked forward to where we would work. My favourite work was serving meals. The boys had to do their own chores on their side of the school.

Figure 3. Dorothy Crate (née James) interviewed outside of Assiniboia's classrooms building, June 2017.

During the first year and week of August 1958, after we arrived at the new school, we asked the nun supervisor if we could go shopping at the T. Eaton Store. She had to ask the principal first and we were allowed to go as long as we returned by 6:00 p.m.

The T. Eaton Store was the company from which we used to make our mail orders from the catalogues, which were sent to all the northern reservations. We used to look forward to receiving these catalogues. But we had no idea where exactly the T. Eaton Store was and nobody offered to drive us there. We had no idea of how to catch a bus either.

Anyway, three girls started walking all the way down Academy Road and came to a bridge, which was the Maryland Bridge. There we saw a store and went inside to ask directions. The storekeeper wrote the street names on a paper and told us the directions, and we were just to follow what he wrote.

We kept walking until we reached the T. Eaton Store, which looked so huge, and we actually were kind of scared to go in, especially when we were in those crazy revolving doors. We went into the store, looked around together, but we didn't even buy anything, as it was all too expensive and fancy. I don't even remember if we went on the elevator. We were kind of scared, although we did end up buying lipsticks and makeup cheap enough for us to afford. We didn't even stop to eat or buy a drink. We kept track of the time, as we had to be back at the school by a certain time.

We walked all the way back to the school again. Later on, we found out the T. Eaton Store had a bargain department. This was our first "adventure" to go shopping.

Our school was situated in the district of River Heights and close to Tuxedo, which we used to call "the highest class area."

Some people used to phone the school, asking for boys who would be interested in some light jobs like shovelling or clearing snow. The boys were excited when it was snowing lots, as they knew they would get a few jobs.

Figure 4. Eaton's Department Store, November 1972.

Same thing for the girls; they would be asked if they would be interested in doing light house-cleaning chores at the homes in the area. My two girlfriends and I were fortunate that we got hired a few times a week and also on weekends to go work in private homes. We sure used to look forward to that, making a few dollars so that we had money for our personal hygiene stuff, treats, and cigarettes.

Then summer holidays began. The Parkhills, the owners of the Parkhill Furniture company, asked us if we wanted to work for them during that summertime. One of my girlfriends and I accepted the job. We were hired by the Parkhills to work at their summer cottage on Coney Island, Lake of the Woods, by Kenora, Ontario. We travelled to the island by boat.

We did not really work hard. We mostly travelled all over the lake, following the Parkhill sailors on the beautiful Lake of the Woods. The Parkhills had one son and two daughters, all of whom were sailors.

We had a pleasant summer, especially riding those big boats. We had our lunches and dinners and suppers right on the boat. It was also fun to watch the sailors. The Parkhills really treated us well and we never regretted working for them. In the fall, we went back to the school. We kept working for the Parkhills during the school years.

There were fifty-three girls and forty-four boys, according to the picture of 1958, of the students at Assiniboia (see Figure 9).

Now it is the year 2016 and in this picture of 1958 I counted that twenty-eight have passed on already, at least of those I knew.

I don't really know how many of them had received their residential school compensation, which was a complicated process, hard to understand with all the forms involved. This is especially true for the northern men and women. It was difficult and many gave up on their claims. As it was, many did not get professional counsellors to help guide them or even counsel them on how to answer all their questions. It was a very emotional and discouraging process. To this day, there is all that unused compensation money. Do we even know what happened to it?

Our teachers were the Grey Nuns, and some white men. I never learned their first names. Our home-economics teacher was a lady. The girls' supervisors were also Grey Nuns. They weren't too strict, nor mean as far as I can remember. We never did encounter any maltreatment.

9

Most of us northern students never went home for the holidays, nor Christmas, because of the distance. We didn't have a Christmas tree, nor presents, nor a beautiful turkey dinner. Our holidays came and went like any regular day. We did not even sleep in, as we woke at our usual time, attended mass as usual, although we did not have classes. Of course, it was always a good feeling for us to see a few of our fellow students going home for the holidays.

I attended Assiniboia Indian Residential School until June 1962. I went somewhere else the following year. I entered the try-out convent for one year at The Pas, Manitoba, but came back to Winnipeg after a year, when I applied to go to Success Business College. While at the college, I had a part-time job at the Shriners Hospital for Sick Children on Wellington Crescent.[2] Lois Parkhill, who I worked for while at Assiniboia, recommended me to go and seek work there. I worked there for five years until I moved on to a different life.

I did not graduate. The difficult time for me was when I had to write the departmental exams, which came from Ottawa. But I managed to pass each year, except when I was in grade eleven. I failed my math and algebra. I was kind of devastated and heartbroken as I had planned to go into nursing. I had completed some subjects in grade eleven. That was it for me. I never did go back to school.

One holiday time, some boys snuck into the girls' dormitory. They got caught and were expelled from the school. One of the guys was from my community—God's Lake. He did not last long at home, some kind of tragic accident, and he died. It was really sad news for us. I also remember there was an Indigenous lady that had a room down the hallway by the girls' side. She spoke the Cree language, but I don't know specifically what kind of work she did at the school, although she was very friendly and we enjoyed talking with her. Many years later, I learned that she was from Fisher River Cree Nation. She is still alive and living in Winnipeg, so I was able to see her a few times.

There was no such thing as "bullying" in our school. I don't really recall any encounters with it, nor fighting, nor arguing among the

Figure 5. Convent, The Pas, Manitoba.

girls. We all got along well and treated each other with kindness and respect.

We wore our own appropriate style of clothes. We used to borrow each other's dresses, blouses, sweaters, et cetera. We did not do any laundry, someone did all of our laundry, but we did our own ironing, as well as tidying up on Saturdays. This was especially to be ready for Sundays.

We would get some visitors on the weekends, especially when we competed in sports like hockey and baseball. That made us look forward to the weekend. We kept busy doing this and that.

The Assiniboia Indian Residential School choir, (above), performed at one of the public sessions of the 1960 Manitoba Indian-Metis conference held in Winnipeg, February 24-27.

Figure 6. The Assiniboia Indian Residential School Choir, 1960.

We also went to study twice on Saturdays and Sundays, too. We had homework to do in all our subject areas, then when we went back to class on Mondays, we would go over the homework with all the students in each grade. Lots of times we did our schoolwork on the boards, too. The students would be on the alert and correct each other when we would make mistakes. We kept all our different subject scribblers, as we used them to study for the final departmental exams, which I think came from Ottawa. I don't really know where they came from. The final exams were never opened until the day or time we wrote them. No marks were counted through the year, just the final exam marks at the end of June, then we would receive our marks in the mail at home and our parents had no idea about our exams or marks or even promotions to the next grade. But, for me, I knew what grade I was to be in when I returned to school in the fall.

I managed to complete grade ten and part of eleven. I really had to study hard in order to pass my classes.

I used to wonder how Phil Fontaine and Jimmy Cook ever passed so easily, as they used to sleep in class, but Sister Tougas never bothered them. Of course, us girls used to whisper to each other, that they were Sister Tougas's pets and that was why she wouldn't wake them up.

Although I didn't graduate from Success Business College, I had enough experience to obtain a receptionist job in the Speech and Hearing Department, where I worked for five years.

Then I took another profession—I got married in the fall of 1968. I have my four children—two girls and two boys. I also now have seven grandchildren and no great-grandchildren as of yet. I have now been living in Fisher River, the home reserve of my late husband, Grenville Crate, for thirty-eight years.

Figure 7. Shriners' Hospital, 1956.

When I first moved to Fisher River, I worked as a homemaker for the Elders, plus as a noon-hour supervisor and substitute teacher at the school. Eventually, I began substituting for the Cree language teacher, Mrs. Lena Murdock, and became her full-time assistant. Then, in 1989, I obtained my "Certification in Cree Language Instruction" through the Continuing Education Department at the University of Manitoba. I was then fortunate to become a Cree language instructor at the school for nursery to grade twelve for twenty years and am still working part-time.

Aside from teaching our Cree language, I have also assisted in developing the first Ochékwisípí Cree dictionary alongside many other Elders in our community. That dedicated work involved many

> "Jerry Wood, a boy from Island lake
> is a good spert who takes part in every-
> thing. He sometimes tries to be serious
> but he doesn't always succeed because his
> smile plays tricks on him."
> By Peter Hart, Norway House
>
> "Dorothy James is seventeen years old
> and stands 5'4". Her charming face
> sends out a very pleasing smile which
> is irresistible. Dorothy originates
> from God's lake."
> By Paul Hart, Norway House
>
> "Dorothy Cook is just back from the
> hospital. We are certainly glad to have
> her back with us because we all love
> her dearly. She is friendly to every-
> one a nd she is smart in her school
> work.
> By Nellie Nicholas, Nelson House

Figure 8. Dorothy James entry in the 1958–59 Assiniboia Newsletter.

hours of meetings, discussions, sharing stories, and even day-to-day living and activities.

In the last twelve years, I have been semi-retired, but I am still working at the school as an Elder to the Cree program, assisting the Cree language teacher as much as I can.

Recent Swampy Cree language projects that I have assisted with include the "BYKI" Cree Language learning program, as well as the latest Cree dictionary and pocket phrase booklet.

It is very rewarding and joyous; however, the fact that our world today is very different from long ago has proven to be challenging as well. I love it and cannot stress enough the importance of passing down our beautiful Swampy-Cree language, given to us by the Creator. We must pass it down to the young people, their children and babies so they can be blessed in life.

Ékosani, Kinanaskomitinawaw.

Figure 9. 1958–59 class photo.

ASSINIBOIA WAS A PLACE OF HOPE FOR US . . .
BUT IT WAS STILL A RESIDENTIAL SCHOOL

Theodore Fontaine
Zaagiing – Sagkeeng First Nation (Fort Alexander, Manitoba)
Attended Assiniboia, 1958–60

Just days before my seventh birthday, I was incarcerated at the Fort
Alexander Indian Residential School. For ten years, 1948 to 1958,
I ate, slept, and worked there, and attended chapel and classes. I lived
there alongside some of my cousins and friends, who became like
family to me. As we looked forward to completing grade nine and
finally escaping the "Fort Alec" school, we were aware that we were
going to be shipped out somewhere else for high school in September.

There was a lot of anticipation, but also doom and gloom, as we
knew many of us would be separated. The Government of Canada
didn't want us to have strong connections to family or friends so we
would be scattered to the winds. Everyone was waiting to learn their
fate. Already we were accustomed to not going home for long lengths
of time. We had been incarcerated in the Fort Alexander school for
ten months every year for an entire decade of our young lives.

The concept of an urban residential school began in the early
fifties, which culminated in the establishment of the Assiniboia Indian
Residential School in Winnipeg in 1958. The first school year was
1958–59. Situated on Academy Road in the heart of River Heights, it
was an experiment in keeping Indian children captive, while advanc-
ing toward the goals of assimilation and isolation from our Indian
language, culture, family, and community.

By the time we were let out of school in June of 1958, my cousins
and I knew we would be going to the Assiniboia school in Winnipeg
and began to anticipate what it would be like. I would gaze out of
the dormitory window, looking to the south, and imagine being in
Winnipeg, 120 kilometres away, not yet thinking about the size of
the city and the complexity of getting around on streets with buses.

Figure 10. Theodore Fontaine on the stairs inside the Assiniboia classrooms building.

We thought we'd get around all right, because during the summers at home, our parents encouraged us to regain our freedom. Sometimes we'd be away from home for two or three days at a time, and they would say, "Ah, they're staying at Uncle JB's," or "You're staying at Auntie Irene's," and not worry about it. In our earliest years before school, before turning seven, we had the freedom to explore the forests, the Winnipeg River and its Canadian Shield rocky banks, and the myriad of trails through the bush that we traversed to visit relatives, to hunt and fish, pick berries, and harvest wild rice.

We knew how to take care of ourselves and how to take care of our families. As a boy of four, five, and six years of age, I helped make sure that the homes of my parents and my Kookum and Mishoom (grandmother and grandfather) were well-supplied with water from the river, firewood, and little animals for the cooking pot, caught with my slingshot and snares. At the age of fifteen, I had no qualms about going to the city.

Three of us, all cousins, Dennis, Richard, and me, decided to check out this new school that summer. We had saved up a little bit of money from working here and there, and we got on the bus in Pine Falls. Our intention was simply to go to Winnipeg to see the school. On the bus, we sat upright on our seats in anticipation. We were on our way, and completely on our own. It took about two hours to get to Winnipeg. As the bus entered the city, we could see all the streets and buildings and started to realize what we'd gotten ourselves into. We got off at the bus depot on Carlton Street. For city folk, it was a well-known, downtown location, but for us it was a little scary, despite our bravado. This was the first time for us to be on our own in this big city.

We knew the school was on Academy Road and so asked for directions on how to go to 621 Academy. Kind strangers would say, "You take this bus, and then another bus." We walked up toward what we now know as Portage Avenue. They used to have those electric buses. They said, "You grab bus 21." I remember that. "You go stand on that corner, and it will take you there. Go stand on the corner across the street from The Bay." They pointed it out. So we stood there and waited.

The bus finally pulled up but we didn't get on. We thought, "It shouldn't be that far; we're going to walk." We waited for it to pull up, and as it pulled out, we followed it. We ran and ran and ran almost until the next bus stop. I don't know where it was, but I think the bus went up a street called Broadway. We watched it go until it disappeared. We waited, and we walked toward where we last saw it. It took us about four or five sprints to get to Assiniboia. Each bus would come and we'd follow it, running until we couldn't see it anymore.

Eventually, we reached Assiniboia—a big, old stone building, really daunting. There was kind of an eerie quiet, but there were workers in there. We didn't go in, but we walked around, sneaking around the building and the yard. We didn't want anyone to know we were there. A couple of workers came out and kind of shooed us away, so we hid behind the building hoping to have a look at the activities in the school, but there was nothing to see, just workers.

They wanted us out of the area but we didn't leave, instead crossing the grounds and ending up on Wellington Crescent. We looked at the big school building from the back. This was where we would eat, sleep, and live. Now we knew what our new school looked like.

We explored around the adjacent building, not knowing it was part of the school, but it was the building where we would have our classes. The classrooms building is now occupied, ironically, by the Canadian Centre for Child Protection. I wonder what involvement they would have had if they were doing this important work when we were in Indian residential schools.

By that time, it was mid-afternoon. The field behind the buildings was huge. We imagined that we would spend our time there, outside, enjoying the freedom of this big grassy area, even though there were high fences all around the property isolating the school and grounds from the community of River Heights. This land would become a haven for us. A place where we could play hockey and baseball, and run, chase each other, and just be kids. Now this land is a designated green space owned by the city.

Figure 11. Theodore Fontaine in the white-sleeved jacket, with his close friends William Paupanekis and Luke Chubb (at right). The photo was taken a few days after their victory in the last All-Indian Residential School hockey tournament played in Brandon, Manitoba, in 1958.

After exploring every part of the property, we started walking back toward where we had come from. By the time we got as far as the Maryland Bridge, it was evening. Somebody had told us that nuns who were going to be teaching at Assiniboia lived in a place called East Gate by the Misericordia Hospital. We ended up there. We thought there might be some kind nuns who would take us in. We tried two doors—knock, knock, knock—but there was no answer. Finally, a nun came out, wondering what we were doing there so late. But she would not accept the urgency of our situation. It was getting late in the day and we thought, "We'd better catch the last bus and try to get home."

So we kept walking, heading back to the bus depot. By the time we got there, it was past six and we had missed the last bus to the Pine Falls area. We sat around for a while and then we were ushered out of the depot by the staff. As we tried to stay, moving to different spots in the bus depot, they would track us down, and say, "We're going to call the police on you."

By the time we tried to get help, it was getting to be dusk. We didn't have anywhere to go or any place to sleep. We had encountered the Maryland Bridge on our way to Assiniboia, and knew it offered the only cover, so we thought we'd find a place to sleep, and headed down below the bridge and that's where we ended up. It was almost dark, and we felt a little panic set in. But we were going to get home somehow, if not today, tomorrow.

We spent a long night underneath the Maryland Bridge—a trio of Indian reserve kids, fifteen- and sixteen-year-old boys who had never stayed unaccompanied in Winnipeg. We tried our best to be comfortable, but endured the night fighting off the heat, mosquitoes, and flies, and the ceaseless hum of traffic. It was a miserable night. We couldn't wait to get out of there.

The next morning, we didn't have a clue what to do. We ended up going back toward the bus depot to catch the morning bus home. Then I found that I didn't have enough money, neither did Dennis. Richard had enough money to buy a ticket, so we said, "You go home.

We'll get there somehow." So, Richard went home on the bus that left at nine in the morning.

I think it cost five cents to use the telephone. Dennis had an older brother, Elmer, who lived in the city, so he phoned his brother, who promptly said, "What the hell are you doing here?" He came down to the bus depot to pick us up and to take Dennis home.

To me he said, "You got any money?" I pulled out the little bit I had, and he said, "You have enough to go on the bus." "Oh boy," I thought, "I'm going to get on the bus to Sagkeeng." What he meant was the city bus. He said, "I'll take you down to the end. I don't live far from the end of Henderson Highway." Henderson Highway was the beginning of the road to get home to Sagkeeng. So, he took us on the bus toward his house, and he and Dennis prepared to get off before the end of the line at the northern edge of the city. He said, "We're going to get off in about five or six stops. You stay on the bus. You go right to the end where it stops and turns around. Get off the bus there and follow that highway. You can hitchhike to Sagkeeng."

I was fifteen years old. I had never hitchhiked before. I didn't even know what it meant. He explained, "You have to make sure you put your thumb out. As cars come along, you stop, you don't keep walking. You stop and put your thumb out." Being a little Indian boy, I was very shy, very backward, and I didn't want to do this. I started to walk and I had a difficult time sticking my hand out, but when I did, I got a ride.

The first ride was up to Lockport. I knew I had to go from Winnipeg to Lockport and then to Beausejour. Highway 12 was quite boring, but I followed the directions quite well and from then on I got rides from a couple of farmers. I'm not saying it happened just like that, one right after another. Sometimes, I had to walk miles and miles before I got a ride.

On that highway to Beausejour, I was walking close to farms. I heard a bunch of dogs barking, and I could see them jumping through the fields toward the highway. I thought, "Oh, now I gotta go around these guys." I broke off a big dry tree branch. It was like I was Moses, walking with a big stick. As I got close to the farm, I could see the dogs yapping away, just looking at me. I headed for the ditch trying to get around them. One came after me and I had to fight him off with the big stick. I finally got away.

I made it home at two or three o'clock in the morning, and my mom was still awake. The lights were on. I could see the relief on my mom's face. She had checked with all the rest of the family members and I was nowhere to be found. Richard of course told them I was in Winnipeg, that he'd left me in Winnipeg. She said, "I knew there was something wrong with my boy," she said. The relief she felt when she saw me was enormous. So ended our adventure to Assiniboia. Satisfied and relieved, we boys stayed home for the rest of the summer.

This story is full of vivid memories for me. I remember so many things we talked about under that bridge, the thoughts and discussions we had when we were fighting off the mosquitoes, our apprehensions, and our good intentions of succeeding in that school. And how we teased Richard, the slow guy and the baby in our group, because we'd have to wait for him when we were chasing the buses. These are etched in my mind. We were so close, only months apart in age. Richard was the youngest, I was in the middle, and Dennis was the oldest. I still feel the closeness we shared, just three young guys, around age fifteen, who didn't know what the hell we were doing.

This story is so indicative of the extreme contrasts I felt at that time in my life. One side was the freedom and joy we experienced as children, being at home safe in the love and comfort of our parents and grandparents. The other was our youthful exuberance for life, jumping into this situation and making it back home again. We knew we were on the verge of adventure and independence as we neared the end of our captivity in Indian residential schools.

In September the Assiniboia Indian Residential School opened. We travelled there by bus from Fort Alexander, arriving within three or four days of kids from other reserves. Our first trip was kind of scary, but we reluctantly accepted that once again we would be confined in an Indian residential school, not knowing what it was going to be like.

Within that first week, we met a Grey Nun. She was in charge of the kitchen and the cooking at Assiniboia. From that first week on, we couldn't believe the way we ate. At the Fort Alexander Indian Residential School, we were always hungry, forcing ourselves to eat cement-like porridge, miserable pieces of hard bread, bacon grease, boiled and raw potatoes. We had to watch and smell the delicious platters of food prepared for the staff but not for us. At Assiniboia, we suddenly experienced healthy food, fresh, tasty, cooked, and plentiful, like we had in our own homes for the short years we lived there. This Grey Nun was Sister Jean Ell.

I learned many years later that the principal, Father Robidoux, gave her complete control of the food budget and Sister Ell took what she had and went to the store. She did her own shopping for the kids. There were about 100 of us as well as all the teachers and staff and workers at the school. She got the food she thought young children needed.

Sister Ell was a real lifesaver. She knew that we had lived for ten years in our previous schools without proper nutrition. In her stories about this critical time in our young lives, she says that Father Robidoux never tried to overrule her or even discuss the food budget with her. She fed us well and made a point of hiring Indigenous kitchen helpers to make bannock and foods that we would have known in our own homes. Everyone at Assiniboia ate the same food from the principal on down the line to the youngest students. She wanted us to be healthy and happy, to be able to learn and to thrive.

As time went on, we found food left out at night, shelved on baking stands for some of the next day's meals. The baking stands were stationed in the kitchen just at the spot where we would pass by every night on our way to the dormitories. We surreptitiously helped ourselves to breads, cakes, and desserts, and gleefully shared them up in our dormitory.

Sister Ell laughs today to hear the story from our side, how we thought we were getting away with sneaking food from the kitchen on our nightly trek to the dormitories, when all along she put it out

23

for us to enjoy and be happily full. She knew we thought we were being clever and she wanted to let us enjoy our imaginary success. She knew it restored a small sense of us having a little bit of control over our own lives.

Figure 12. Daniel Highway, Sister Ell, Theodore Fontaine, and Father Alarie.

She tells me the story of one night leaving an unfinished plate of cake on the stand, making sure it was right where we would pass by, and knowing of course that it would disappear. The next morning, as we passed by in line going in for breakfast, Sister Ell took her usual spot at the front to bid us good morning. She happily greeted us and as she greeted one of my close friends, in line behind me, she joyfully asked him, "Was the cake good?" My friend started to respond, "It was very good," then began to blush and stammer to save himself. I often tease my friend about this incident, and he still insists, with a shy grin, "It wasn't me, boy." Sister Ell and I still enjoy talking about his reaction at being found out. Today she is a close and treasured friend. My wife and I visit her frequently and admire her greatly.

It should be noted that Sister Ell was about twenty-one years old when she was the head cook at Assiniboia, only about five years older than the boys and girls who depended on her so greatly. Her kindness, playful sense of humour, and innate use of psychology have forever sustained me. She went on to a brilliant career as a psychiatric social worker and has been honoured for her enormous and lifelong contributions to social services in Winnipeg and Canada. She was astonished to find out very recently that Father Robidoux had been pressured to defend her expenditures multiple times over those years, but he never once told her to cut back, or that any questions had ever been raised.

The classic building housing the Assiniboia Indian Residential School was built in 1915 at 621 Academy Road at the south footing of the St. James Bridge. It was a place of refuge throughout its noteworthy history, serving as the Children's Home of Winnipeg until 1945, then becoming a convalescent home for Canadian veterans. It served as the Assiniboia Indian Residential School from 1958 to 1973, then part of it was used as a counselling office where First Nations students who lived in Winnipeg could come for counselling and a bus pass so they could attend other schools in the city. The main school building that was home to so many was demolished in 1985 to make way for construction of the RCMP forensic laboratory.

At that time, all of the old artifacts from the Assiniboia school were put into storage. Survivors were never contacted about this, and when the school was dismantled, we thought everything in storage would be preserved. Instead, almost everything was destroyed. Maybe the government's intention was to leave no trace of the school and no trace of us.

I can only tell you about two examples of what was saved and why these items did not disappear. In the mid-1970s, as the school was being demolished, artifacts from the school were being hauled out to be taken to the garbage dump. A woman who worked in the counselling office was Muriel McLeod, and she saw what was being done to the historic evidence of the school. She managed to save the fine embroidery work of the young women from the first few years of the residential school. These young women were taught embroidery, although this was a skill most would have learned at home. But their hand-sewn embroidery pieces were put into a pile at the front door where a garbage truck would pick up these and other leftovers from the school. Muriel McLeod salvaged these pieces. Otherwise they would have been forever lost in a landfill.

The second artifact saved was the original picture of the 1958–59 class of the Assiniboia Indian Residential School. I just happened to be at the counselling centre around the same time that Mrs. McLeod found the embroidery. I was then living in the Northwest Territories and came home for the summer. I dropped in at the counselling centre to recall my experiences and feelings for Assiniboia. Lying in that same pile by the door, that pile destined for the garbage, was our class picture. It was in awful condition. It was the original 1958 school picture, with the original individual photos of each of the ninety-seven students with Father Robidoux. We affectionately called him "Weese."

I picked it up amidst the shattered glass and broken frame. A security guard was watching me as I stood with it in my hands, standing right at the door. He must have seen the tears in my eyes as he nodded permission for me to save that picture. That picture is one of my most prized possessions. I have made reproductions of it for everyone I can find who attended Assiniboia, especially those who were in that first-year class with me. A print is mounted in our former classrooms building, the only surviving structure of our school. It was produced with honour and respect for the Survivors of Assiniboia by the Canadian Centre for Child Protection, and is proudly displayed on the wall where their workers fight child exploitation and child abuse every day.

Assiniboia was a place of hope for us, coming from lives of deprivation and abuse at remote residential schools. But it was still a residential school for Indian children, far away from family and home. We ate, slept, and lived there, attended classes, and played outside within the confines of tall wire fences. We were both protected and isolated from the white population. The community of River Heights had been thrust in the forefront of the government's strategy to ensure that Indian children would be kept from the influences of our families, although some residents didn't want Indian kids in their community.

This was evident in our reality within days of our arrival, as we were lying in our beds in the twilight of the evening about 9:00 or 9:30 p.m. The boys' dormitories, each with twenty-five to thirty boys, were roused up by a great commotion outside. We quietly climbed to the third-floor windows to see young white people going by on Academy Road doing their best to mimic Indian war whoops as mischaracterized on television. Each little group of five or six was letting us know what they thought about us being there. I often wonder if I ever encounter any of these individuals in my life as a resident of Winnipeg.

There were other disturbing incidents intended to belittle and demean our worth as Indians. The leadership of our principal, Father Robidoux, was low-key, but he went about addressing the cross-cultural ignorance of our new community. One evening, he directed our supervisor to approach five or six of the older boys, including me, to tell us that some white boys outside had been seen trying to sneak into the girls' dormitory through the back way and up the adjacent trees. He asked us to pull those boys down and get them into the building. In the dark, we couldn't get them all but we brought three or four to the principal's parlour.

Back in the dormitory later, we heard the crunching of tires on the gravel driveway at the front entrance. A couple of black and white police vehicles pulled up and parked by the entrance, next to a few expensive vehicles with parents getting out and going up the short steps into the front entrance of the school. We were interrupted by the lights being flashed on by the supervisor, proclaiming that Father Robidoux was receiving "visitors" and we were all to go to bed. I'm not aware of the results of this, but hopefully some of those young men have redeemed themselves over the years.

Students from Assiniboia also faced a barrage of racial epithets while competing in hockey, baseball, football, and track and field meets. In one sense, it prepared us for the barrage that continued into our adult years.

Competing in hockey, we were quite used to facing incidents of racism during our early years in residential schools on reserves, playing against local white town teams. We found it no different playing teams in Winnipeg and area communities. The first contingent of hockey players at Assiniboia, a team coached by our supervisor Luc, was almost unbeatable. A number of our players should have later joined the ranks of professional hockey, had they survived.

Figure 13. Theodore Fontaine and Oliver Nelson, c. 1958–59.

One incident, almost typical, was with a team from a town near Winnipeg. It was obvious we were on our way to another victory when, with just a few minutes left, an altercation took place close to our net. Oliver, one of our better defencemen, got tangled up with one of their skaters. Jostling and anger took over and an opposing player came flying out of their bench and blindsided Richard, another of our defencemen. It became a free-for-all brawl on the ice.

After all the cursing, yelling, and punching, calm was restored. The story emerged that the adult player who charged Richard was a local priest playing for the town team. He had incited the hate-based, unnecessary confrontation, encouraged by the verbal onslaught of the fans. Of course, we had no family or friends close enough to attend our games and cheer for us. Some of us would often comment about this incident and wonder what that priest would say at his Sunday sermons. We would hope that sometime we would meet him again, perhaps on a mutual reconciliation path.

Most of my friends from Assiniboia are now gone. Of those who survived Indian residential schools, many died early in life, struggling to overcome abuses, sorrow, and losses, experiencing lifelong effects and impacts. Those who couldn't survive were lost, with all they could have offered and accomplished, not only for their families and communities, but for Canada. Yet for many, the Assiniboia Indian Residential School was a little oasis in the turbulent seas of the Indian residential school era.

Figure 14. Morgan and Theodore Fontaine inside Assiniboia's classrooms building.

In a turn of destiny sixty years ago, I met my future wife while clearing the sidewalk of her family home when I was at the Assiniboia Indian Residential School and she was a young River Heights girl. Father Robidoux had seen that some of the older boys would sneak across Academy Road to a little store that was like a confectionery. With whatever little money we could scrounge from visiting family members, we would buy gum, chips, chocolate bars, and candy. Little did we know he watched us from his office window.

Realizing that we didn't usually have any money, Father Robidoux, in his kindness and vision, determined that we were highly motivated to earn some money. So he allowed a few of us to venture out to homes near the school to offer some help by shovelling driveways and sidewalks. What a joy, the prospect of going out into the neighbourhood, experiencing freedom from school. Three of us set off, myself, Joe Guy, and Charles Edward (Teddy). Soon feeling more adventurous, we began to wander farther than the boundary that had been approved for us.

I believe that Father Robidoux was very progressive and worked to enhance the interactions between ourselves and the community. It paved the way for common understanding and acceptance. He later became the bishop of a northern diocese, and tragically died in a plane crash. I still remember and bless him in my prayers.

Our bravery and newfound freedom took us a few blocks out of limits one late afternoon, after school. We ended up standing on Renfrew Street outside a home with a sidewalk not yet cleared. We were all somewhat hesitant and a little awkward, but I was pushed forward to knock on the door. I knocked timidly and jumped back a bit as the door opened. Out emerged a lovely white lady, nicely dressed, who greeted us with a puzzled, "May I help you?" I still remember her British accent. She seemed to be wondering who were these scruffy Indian kids at her door. Her young daughter came to peer at us through the door, then whispered, "I think it's those Indian boys from that school down the road."

With permission, we shovelled the sidewalk, then gobbled down the cookies and hot chocolate she offered us. Twenty years later, when I was Chief of Sagkeeng First Nation, that young girl would resurface in my life as a communications professional at the Department of Indian Affairs, designated to help me and a Council of Chiefs in public information and media initiatives. Years later, we would form a lifelong partnership that is soon approaching forty years. A number of good things came out of my time at Assiniboia Indian Residential School, and meeting my future wife became my biggest reconciliation.

In this last phase of my life, dedicated to public awareness and reconciliation, I visit the Canadian Centre for Child Protection often. They welcome me with all the love, understanding, and tenderness that I missed so desperately during my twelve years of incarceration in Indian residential schools. I park at the edge of the playing fields where we used to play hockey and baseball. I am thankful that the City of Winnipeg has preserved this precious land. The little hillside by the railway tracks is sometimes filled with the laughter of children sledding and, in the summer, the fields resound with the joy of baseball games.

When it's quiet, the spirits of our lost souls gather there, lingering with me, a little bit thankful and a little bit heartbroken. I smudge and pray for them. It is my privilege as a Survivor to give voice to these memories, to work to preserve this history and this space that is sacred to us. I pledge that these innocent children are not forgotten though their voices were silenced long ago.

Figure 15. Theodore Fontaine, Caroline Perreault, and Betty Ross at the Assiniboia playing field, 2019.

Figure 16. Adeline Raciette and Emily [Emma] Bone study on the lawn of the Assiniboia Indian Residential School, Winnipeg, Manitoba, c. 1958.

SIHKOS' STORY:
ASSINIBOIA INDIAN RESIDENTIAL SCHOOL[3]

Jane Glennon (née McCallum)
Peter Ballantyne Cree Nation, Saskatchewan
Attended Assiniboia, 1958–61

Upon my arrival in the fall of 1958 at the Assiniboia Indian Residential School in Winnipeg, it wouldn't be long before I once again found myself disappointed with the way things were run.

In my late teens by this point, I was a reluctant student. But the parish priest and my parents never wavered: both were still firm that I continue my education so that I might fulfil the potential they saw in me.

"You are smart, and learn quick," I'll always remember my mother saying. "You can become something and have a good life," she'd urge.

Speaking of potential, after my first two schools, I thought this experience might prove more modern and uplifting. But the same basic rules and regulations were in place at Assiniboia. There was one difference: the order to which the sisters belonged, namely, the Grey Nuns. Along with the Oblate Fathers, they administered the school, in cooperation with the federal government. There was even an Aboriginal nun. Some students related to her, but, beyond being understanding and helpful in some areas, she couldn't really obtain any concessions for us. Yet more disappointment, I guess.

At Assiniboia, I was mostly preoccupied with trying to get good grades but at the same time got very homesick, even if I was now older. That sense of forced isolation from loved ones was one shared by many of my classmates. On the edge of this fenced yard where we all played baseball, my girlfriends and I endlessly walked and reminisced about our homes or boyfriends. Many years later, I revisited those schoolgrounds: the path we used to walk, week after week, was still visible.

There were times that I tried to act on my homesickness. Once, a couple of friends and I tried to run away. We didn't get very far, however: possessing neither the money nor the courage to venture into the big city, we soon turned back. Another time, a friend from my reserve and I missed home so much we protested by locking ourselves in the bathroom, refusing to go to class. Eventually, the principal came and talked us out of there by persuading us that it was important that we continue our education. Looking back, I'm thankful he did, as both my friend and I went on to make something of ourselves by following a learning path.

But then, school wasn't just about books for me: it was also about boys. Of course, at Assiniboia, having boyfriends consisted of smiling across the dining hall and waving. (Still, some may have stolen a little kiss or two in a forbidden part of the school now and then.)

Figure 17. Assiniboia Indian Residential School Students Pictured with French Ambassador Francis Lacoste, c. 1959.

Secret letters or notes were also a way of communicating young love. A relationship I had with a Cree boy at Assiniboia was memorable in part because love notes I'd written got snatched up somehow by a teacher. When I consequently got taken to the principal, I knew I had to think fast.

Believing myself to be the rather convincing sort, I pleaded with the principal not to read my notes in front of the whole student body. It took some effort, but on the promise that I would never do such a thing ever again, I managed to succeed. Such theatrics over the foolish musings of a boy and girl caught up in innocent puppy love!

Not so loving was the rivalry between Cree students and our more numerous Saulteaux/Ojibway classmates. (At my previous schools, conflict between the Cree and Dene children was less obvious.) Tensions never really escalated beyond the verbal at Assiniboia: the only scars that came out of it were hurt egos. When those negative comments did come our way, we Crees retaliated by outsmarting our Ojibway counterparts through other channels, such as games or academics.

* * *

By spring time, some of the girls would literally count the days until we were headed home. After ten straight months of forced separation from our families, we were deeply relieved to rejoin them. The happiness I felt when the plane touched down and I could once again see the smiling faces of my waiting parents is something I'll never forget.

My mother would try to make a special meal to welcome us home. I remember one time she had cooked Kraft Dinner—not nearly so common then as it is now—attempting to stretch it so that we would all have some to enjoy. Simple as it was, to me the meal was fantastic. I understood that my parents did not have much, but they tried their best to let us know that we were special.

These all-too-short summer holidays over, I dreaded the idea of going back to school and being away from my family for so many months. It never got easier. One year, I hid under a big wooden bed to avoid going back. When the parish priest and the Indian agent first came for me, they told my parents that I had lots of potential and shouldn't waste it. Then they said that it was against the law to hold back a school-age child. Unable to win my parents over by persuasion, these officials turned to threats to make me go back.

* * *

Not all of my troubles were confined to the grounds of the residential school. In fact, what I am about to tell you took place while I was at home on holidays. It is the story of my first experience of sexual abuse. That dreadful summer, I was about eleven years of age, maybe younger: I'm not entirely sure anymore. As we did every season, our family's tradition was to either go camping or head to my father's commercial fishing spot. Sometimes, this expedition would grow to include friends and extended family.

At night, we'd all share a tent: sleeping arrangements consisted of me being sandwiched by my parents on one side, a man (one I've decided not to name here) on the other. As the evening wore on, he must have moved closer and closer into the space I was sleeping. I cannot say exactly what happened next because I don't remember, but I do know with certainty that I had been sexually abused, for when I woke up I was hurting and wet between my legs.

I was scared to tell my mother about it because I thought she would not believe me: this man was someone my mother liked very much. For the longest time, I was angry at her for not hearing anything while I was being abused. I even came to believe that she did hear something but chose to say nothing. However, reasoning that such a thing would be too horrible to do to one's young child, I let the notion drop.

While my mother was alive, I never had the courage to ask her about what took place. Making it worse was how this man subsequently tried to lay the blame on me for the abuse, ridiculing me and calling me names. I used to feel awful and mad but, again, did not have the courage to tell anyone about what he'd done to me.

As I got older, I tried to forget. I even prayed for my mother and this man, right up until their deaths. With professional help, I have slowly come to terms with what happened, to the point where I can now share my story with you today. I do so knowing there are more and more revelations of such abuse, with media reports revealing its prevalence among Aboriginal and non-Aboriginal families alike. I've also heard similar stories first-hand from people that I know well. And yet, due to a sense of shame and people's tendency to somehow lay the blame on themselves, no one reports this abuse, leaving them to carry around this misplaced guilt alone for years.

* * *

At around fourteen, I got a job working summers at a fish plant; my starting wage was eighty cents an hour. I was part of a crew whose task it was to pick lice-like worms out from fish fillets. We'd clean the fillets on a glass table that was lit from below so we could better make out the worms. Thinking back, I am sure the boss was breaking some sort of labour laws by hiring underage girls. However, because I was finally earning some money to help the family, I didn't ask questions.

After I left the Assiniboia Indian Residential School, the parish priest made arrangements for me to join Assumption House, an organization that trained lay missionaries up north in The Pas, Manitoba. I must admit that was never my ambition. It's clear to me now that the priest had always wanted me to leave the reserve and, for him, this was a good reason for doing so.

When I got to Assumption House, I was shocked to learn that I in fact had been slated to finish my grade eleven and twelve at none other than Guy Hill Indian Residential School! It had since been renovated to accommodate high-schoolers, and I was left no choice but to start classes at a place I thought I'd never set foot in again. Though the surroundings were familiar, the teaching staff came from a different order of nuns. I felt invisible to them. I also felt trapped as I revisited my memories all over again. Most of all, I felt profoundly alone.

Surrounded by nothing but white faces, I heard not a single word of kindness or encouragement from these nuns. Unable to stand this unkind, uncaring environment for more than a few months, I was done. Though I'm sure it disappointed a few people, I'd made up my mind: I would quit school and the missionary training in order to return home to my reserve.

IT'S A WHOLE DIFFERENT WAY OF LIFE

Caroline Perreault (née Seymour)
Waanibiigaaw – Hollow Water, Manitoba
Attended Assiniboia, 1958–62

Transcribed from an oral interview.[4]

I started my residential schooling at the Fort Alexander Indian Residential School. I remember being picked up at home. When I got to Fort Alexander, my brother-in-law took me across the river in a boat to go to that school. The Oblates who ran the school said, "We are going put you with a family right now because we are kind of full." I found all of these changes very terrifying, since I was away from home for the first time.

When I started at Fort Alexander Indian Residential School, I cried the first night. There were a lot of young girls and they were very quiet. After crying the first few nights, I decided that I had to make this work.

I used to talk to myself inside my head. If there was something that upset me, I would pray about it.

What I recall most is the loneliness. I came from a family that was very close, and to not have any contact with them was very difficult.

I soon decided to be friendlier. It was difficult to make friends.

I was told I had to be on the hockey team. I said, "I don't want to play hockey. I don't want to get hit." I wasn't too keen on playing. I was also really shocked when they put us all together to have a shower. I found that very stressful. It was the same at Assiniboia.

The daily routine was attending morning mass before our chores began. I was raised Catholic at home so I was used to prayers.

At Assiniboia, we were all up by 6:00 a.m., getting ready so we could be downstairs in the chapel by 7:00 a.m. Every morning we were in the chapel and had breakfast before we did our chores. At Fort Alexander, meals were always the same food, usually a lot of moose meat. At Assiniboia, some of us were assigned to wait on the staff, to serve them and bring the food to them. I used to look at the food and think, "How come our food is different?"

The school taught us that the only way to succeed is to concentrate on what you want to be and study.

After Fort Alexander, I attended Assiniboia. I started in January of the same year it opened (1958–59). I had to work extra hard because of that to be able to pass most of my subjects. I took notes from everybody. Every Saturday, I went and studied the notes that I borrowed from the other students, just trying to catch up. I wanted to succeed.

A lot of students, like me, came from very poor families. When I was at Assiniboia, I asked the school if they could put me to work somewhere so I could buy toothpaste or whatever small items I needed. Because I never had any pocket money, I never went out on gatherings outside the school grounds.

Figure 18. Caroline Perreault in front of Assiniboia Indian Residential School, c. 1959.

I was one of the lucky people that learned very quickly. I grasped things and they would stay with me. I started at Assiniboia that first year, and at the school elections I was elected to be a leader to do things like serve as a moderator and be a public speaker. I did that. And I helped guide others on how to speak. I was very comfortable with that. I was more confident in myself, I guess. Determined might be the best word. I was determined to succeed. I would tell myself, "I can do this. I can do this."

At Assiniboia, the girls were all on one side of the campus and the boys on the other. A lot of the students who went to Assiniboia have passed. But I remember trying to be friendly, and I would manage to get close to some fellow students, whom I made friends with.

I remember some of the trips I went on while at Assiniboia. I was involved in a play that we put on, and we also had a dance group. We acted in a small theatre group, and I was the head nun in a play. I had the chance to imitate those nuns by being bossy. We performed it at one school, and we went to a gathering and put on this play and everybody liked it so much that we ended up performing shows in different areas in the city and at other schools.

I was also involved in the girls' baseball team at Assiniboia. But I don't recall much about it. I was more into the arts, classic stories, plays, and music. That was me. I was not into this sport, being a baseball hitter or batter or whatever.

Figure 19. Caroline Perreault and the Assiniboia Girls' Baseball Team, c. 1959.

The principal was good to me, but then I followed the rules as much as I could, because I knew that was the only way to stay out of trouble.

He was driving us to get educated, pushing us like he did. "If you want to succeed, you study and work hard at it," he would say. If you listened, you stayed on track, which I did. But a lot of the kids wanted to go home and be with their parents or families. A lot of them dropped out by December that first year. A few students went home for Christmas holiday and never came back. They missed their homes and their culture and where they lived. It was like black and white, coming from the country and coming to this. It's a whole different way of life. The structure, waking up at a certain time, meeting at a certain time, having a break at a certain time, breakfast, lunch, and supper at a certain time. That was the structure, every day, day in and day out.

The students missed their families. The affection they had received from their families was gone. You weren't allowed to touch, or to give or receive affection. I think that was the hardest part for all of us, lacking that affection that we had from our parents and our families, or brothers and sisters. Back home, the older ones always took care of the smaller ones.

TWO HUNDRED AND TWENTY-TWO MILES FROM HOME

Valerie T. Mainville

Couchiching First Nation, Ontario
Attended Assiniboia, 1962–67

A Poem to Assiniboia Residential School,
Winnipeg, Manitoba

These were my high-school years
twelve to seventeen.
I am a Survivor who left home
at twelve, through no choice of my own
to attend the residential school
two hundred and twenty-two miles from home.

I left my homeland
where I attended eight years of grade school at another residential
school.
While in Winnipeg
I loved volleyball but wasn't chosen for football cheerleader,
I skated in minus-40-degree Fahrenheit weather, treaded snow
to my knees,
I tried curling to no avail.

We built an ice sculpture buffalo,
loved bowling,
met wonderful lifelong friends,
learned the sciences,
yearned for mail,
two hundred and twenty-two miles from home.

On outings,
I went to Elvis shows at downtown movie theatres,
danced every dance I knew,

sang songs on the radio,
found fashion at Portage Mall,
wore miniskirts, trench coats, and knee-high boots.

I discovered poetry,
sang in the choir,
learned foreign languages
and cultures;
whereas, I barely knew mine,
two hundred and twenty-two miles from home.

I was warm,
earned money,
but was so restricted,
always reprimanded
for being me—
silenced by the nuns.

I wasn't allowed to play,
was shushed in dormitories,
lived with regulatory regimentation,
was watched like a hawk, with imaginary boundaries,
never allowed to date
or rarely talk with the opposite sex.

I was denied freedom of speech
by religious acts,
always learning their new ways,
never practising ours.
I wanted to type versus take a language,
two hundred and twenty-two miles from home.

There was no contact with home
except for letters and holidays, ten months of the year.

I counted the days to return
to freedom at home.
We were shaped to be ourselves today
but never forgot our ancestry.

I could not see the control
of not moving in freedom from corporal punishment.
We prayed a lot but why?
I longed to be home, but couldn't;
I was silenced then, not now,
when I was two hundred and twenty-two miles from home.

VALERIE MAINVILLE (VAL)
AMBITION TEACHER
HOBBY COLLECTING PICTURES
DISPOSITION SMILING
SPORTS SWIMMING & BOWLING

Figure 20. Valerie Mainville's portrait in the Keewatin Yearbook, 1966.

ON THE WHOLE, IT WAS A GOOD EXPERIENCE

Mabel Horton (née Hart)

Nisichawayasihk Cree Nation (Nelson House, Manitoba)

Attended Assiniboia, 1962–67

Transcribed from an oral interview.

I was in Assiniboia from 1962. I was eleven or twelve years old when I began, and I left in 1967. So, I was there for grades eight, nine, ten, eleven, and twelve.

It was quite the experience, but in a good way for me—that is to say, I wasn't physically abused, sexually abused, or otherwise. There was an incident, but it was nothing that I would report to the Truth and Reconciliation Commission.[5] On the whole, it was a good experience, and that's what I want to share, especially with the youth of today.

My parents instilled in us the importance of education. My brothers and my sister were also at Assiniboia. We weren't here all at the same time, because my brother was part of the initial group of students. Before that, I was in Guy Hill Residential School, which is near OCN (Opaskwayak Cree Nation), in The Pas area.

My parents were very instrumental in what they wanted us to do with education in our lives, for the future, because they knew it was very important. They encouraged us to continue while they were alive. They wanted to see us graduate and go on to success-ful degrees, careers, whatever, and make good lives for ourselves. They hadn't had the same opportunity. They were very traditional—and that was what they knew and they were good at what they did. They were really good parents.

My dad did not believe in welfare, as it is now, and he was deter-mined to work all his life. And he did.

I'm married and I have two children and two grandsons. We also instill the importance of education in our children. It's important to address the youth, to encourage them just to keep going, despite all

Front row: (L. to R.) Josephine Robinson, Billy Flett, Sister Tougas, Audrey McPherson, Mary Edna Flett.
Back row : (L. to R.) Rita Nanowin, Bernice Henry, Bertha Fontaine, Bella Hart.

Front row: (L. to R.) Phillip Castel, Mabel Hart, Agnes Nanowin, Sister B. Brisebois, Valerie Mainville, Cecilia York, Moses Okimow.
Second row:(L. to R.) Richard Courchene, Christina Crate, Brenda Balfour, Lillian Mason, Delphine Houle, Dolores Nanie, Edwin Bruyere, William Merasty.
Third row: (L. to R.) Saul Day, George Ballantyne, Alphius Wilson, Leonard McKay Sr., Stanley Moussesu, Lalio Mamageesic, Joseph Cook, Not shown: Cameron Wood.

Figure 21. Faculty Page from the 1964 Assiniboia Yearbook.

the problems that they run across. I know we were in a boarding residential school and we were segregated and the whole bit, but now the current generation is out there facing all the challenges of today—the social media, bullying, and the rest of it.

Figure 22. David Montana Wesley, Mabel Horton, and Betty Ross, 2015.

My parents also instilled in us the value of education. They took time out to come and see us at school before we returned home in the summer. We went home for two months, and at Christmas time we went home by train from here all the way to northern Manitoba, near Thompson. Thompson wasn't there when I was going to school. And then we went by plane—I don't know if you know what a Bombardier is, but anyway we went by Bombardier. And it was quite an experience, because you can't sit facing forward. You have to sit facing sideways and the windows were in front. There were four of us. And you got motion sickness. It was just bump, bump, bump.

We were so happy to be home when we saw the lights of our communities. There was no electricity then, just little fuel oil lamps; but you could see the lights and we were so happy. I mean, it was home, right? We were happy to see our folks.

Like I said, my siblings were with me in the years I was at Assiniboia, but we didn't see each other all the time because the boys were on one side, the girls were on the other, and my sister had her own group of friends, but at least I knew she was around. And then they let us visit our brother in what they called the parlour, which was near the entrance of the office, on Sundays. We'd sit in our little Sunday clothes, and sit with our hands on our lap type of thing—it was totally unreal.

At least we saw each other. And we would laugh and hug, and fool around and stuff. We were supervised.

After I graduated, I made many friends, and I have lifelong friends from Assiniboia.

After I left high school, I went to nursing school in Winnipeg. It was supposed to be hospital training, but it turned out to be one of the hospital groups. Instead of three-year hospital training, we completed two-and-a-half. Then, Red River College opened and it was only two years for nurses—regular RNs (Registered Nurses)—although they started doing just the degree courses, which are four years. And it was, like, you had no choice. Except in Manitoba, they did have LPNs (Licensed Practical Nurses). I think to this day they still allow LPNs.

I finished that and went nursing in Winkler, Manitoba, which is very Mennonite. There's a good story there. I wouldn't put it on this record.

Next off I went up north to Norway House Indian Hospital, as they called it then, and then later to Cross Lake, God's Narrows, and the Territories, as a nurse.

I was an outpost nurse for many years.

We went to the Territories after our children were born, and then we came down to the south—well, it's still the north, but we call it south—in Thompson. I did public health there for a number of years—ten years—and enjoyed it very much. Then I switched and worked for a political organization; and I went into political analysis with a focus on health. I only retired four years ago. I was at the Assembly of Manitoba Chiefs for ten years. I was into e-health, electronic health records, and telehealth programs. So that was important, because we had a lot of meetings with the federal government, the province, and Winnipeg—so that was an experience.

What I'm trying to say is that it's really important, to yourself, your family, your community, and leaders to get your education and stick with it, and there are lots of benefits as a person, and you make money—that helps. You get to live in nice homes, like I do. I'm grateful for what I have. I live in Headingley, right by the river, no mortgages, and that type of thing, so it's lovely. But what I want to stress to the youth is this:

We have two children. Our oldest son will be thirty-eight in July, and our daughter is thirty-six. Right now, they're both in Canada, so it's good. Myles, our oldest, is a medical doctor and he's a neurologist, specialized in stroke care. He went many years to university—thirteen or fifteen years with residency and all the rest of it. I think he is a role model for youth and our community. *Achimowina* [a newspaper for the Nisichawayasihk Cree Nation] invited him to speak and be on the newsletter; and all the chiefs he's known are very proud of him. Of course, we all are.

He has two little boys; Henry is four-and-a-half and Archer is three. Our daughter-in-law is non-Indigenous and comes from Toronto, but she's very interested in having them learn their language.

Whenever I see them, or we do FaceTime, I try to speak my language to them. It might sound hilarious, but they try to say it. I know it's important to try to reach them before five years old. But they live in Vancouver. They were learning Mandarin in daycare. I thought, "Okay, that's important too, but I'd love them to learn my Cree language."

My husband is from an English background. Well, he's from England. But he encourages our traditional activities. I do a lot of traditional activities with sweats and stuff like that, and my children have gone through that as well, with their vision quests, traditional names, and ceremonies.

Our daughter finally got to Tofino, all the way from Costa Rica. I went to meet her in Guatemala, and we went to Mexico and the States. I'm still having nightmares about our travel. But she is totally opposite to her brother. She's into holistic, alternative medicine, and she's into yoga and all the rest of it. They're both in medicine in a different way, and I'm very proud of them both.

As I said, I wanted to do this for the youth—not to give up. There's hope out there for them to do whatever they want to do. I know it sounds like a cliché, but you just have to persevere.

I was not going to speak in public about all of this, but I thought that it was important to have it recorded; and, not to appear that I'm bragging about things, but I think that as Survivors we need to tell our stories for our youth, and actually for the non-Aboriginal people to know that we do it. I have a Master's in Public Administration in the area of health, and I obtained that at the tender age of sixty before I retired.

All those years we were in the North, I did distance education. Some of you will laugh, I know, but it was through cassette recorders. We got the stuff in the mail. We did it, and we sent our stuff back on tape and written. There was no email nor Internet at the time, so—as I said—you have to try, and you have to keep going. That's very important.

So, thank you for asking us. The Class of '67, we were from Assiniboia.

Cont'd   GRADE XI-A

Valerie Mainville. Valerie comes from Fort Frances, Ontario. We elected her as Secretary-Treasurer of our Student Council, and We're not sorry. You're doing a wonderful job, Val. Keep it up! Besides writing the minutes, Valerie is a studious worker in school and I bet she is even counting the minutes until exam time!

Alphius Joseph Wilson. Alphius was born on January 4, 1948. He is a six-footer weighing 140 pounds. He is a gentleman from Norway House and his ambition is to be an Indian Agent.

Richard Courchene. Fort Alexander is fortunate to be represented by Richard or "Ricky" as he is called by his friends. Ricky is adorned with brown curly hair and sparkling brown eyes. This handsome fellow plans to be a teacher and teach in his own reserve. I am sure you will succeed, Richard!

Agnes Nanowin. "Aggie" is a product of Matheson Island Manitoba. She is a seventeen year-old, standing five feet four inches. She has keen interest in all her school subjects and at the moment, she has not made up her mind yet, whether to become a nurse or a teacher. Best wishes to you, Aggie!

Cameron Wood. Cameron, or Butch is tall, dark, and handsome and is from St. Theresa Point, Manitoba. He hopes to become a forest ranger, and knowing him I know he will succeed.

Brenda Belfour. A good-looking girl from Norway House, Manitoba. Brenda wishes to be a teacher in the near future. For a hobby, she enjoys playing records and takes active part in sports. Her favourite expression is "shucks" especially at a time of crisis.

Philip Castel. A gentleman from Pukatawagon, Manitoba is Mr. Castel. Although he is quiet, he is always seen in class and really takes his work seriously. His ambition is to be a conservation officer. Best wishes to you, Philip.

George Ballantyne. The gentleman who works hard and who is going to make his hometown very proud of him is none other than George Ballantyne. His great desire is to be a music composer. His favourite subject is English and favourite sport is football which he plays tremendously well. If you ever hear an "ARROOO!" , don't be alarmed that is only George's favourite expression. His way of passing time is singing to himself and his favourite food is sunny-side up eggs.

Saul Day. A very promising young lad from Sandy Lake, Ontario is Mr. Saul Day. With his determination and talents he is sure to succeed in any career. His hobbies are reading, mice-hunting, and frog-legs collecting.

Mabel Hart. A charming young lady of fifteen has been shipped from Nelson House, Manitoba. Her favourite saying is "My Goodness!" and her favourite foods are bannock and fried meat. Mabel plans to take nursing. We wish you good luck, Mabel.

Christina Crate. Christina is a fine, pretty girl from Norway House, Manitoba. Her ambition is to be a registered nurse and I am sure she will be a success. She is a Rolling

cont'd

Figure 23. Description of Mabel Horton (née Hart) and her grade eleven classmates from the 1964 Assiniboia Newsletter.

YOU GOTTA KEEP GOING . . .
NO MATTER WHAT

David Montana Wesley
Longlac, Ontario
Attended Assiniboia, 1963–65

Transcribed from an oral interview.

I will tell you about how I became a student at Assiniboia. It was a mystery to me where I was going as a high-school student. I was fifteen when I was called by the Government of Canada—it was Indian Affairs at the time. Like I said, I didn't know where I was going. I had other siblings who were going on the same bus.

There was a high school that was fifty kilometres away from where I lived in Longlac, and I thought that we were going to high school in Geraldton, but the bus kept going and going. Then we didn't know where we were going.

We stopped in—back then it was called Port Arthur, Ontario. It's now called Thunder Bay. The schools were full there.[6] The bus took us to Fort Frances; there was a residential school there.[7] When we arrived, that school was full. Once again, we kept going.

We ended up in Sioux Narrows, Ontario. There was a school there. I think it was called Father Moss. It was just a small school. Two of my siblings were taken off of the bus. They were younger. I had three other sisters with me. We continued to Winnipeg. That's how I ended up being a high-school student at Assiniboia.

We had no idea that we were going to a residential school. We thought we were going to a regular high school. Of course, at the time, my parents didn't know. They told my parents that their children were going to a high school, thinking that we were going fifty kilometres away, but 800 kilometres later we ended up at Assiniboia.

Of course, being just young people, we were bewildered and at first very scared, because it was a new city. We were coming from Longlac to the metropolis of Winnipeg. Of course, you get scared, eh?

But, once I realized that we were at a Native school, well, it felt better, you know, being with your own people. But you still have that feeling of being scared. You're a stranger in town.

We slowly settled into our new environment.

Of course, we didn't realize that it was a girls' and boys' school. I was separated from my two sisters. I missed talking to my sisters. Back then you couldn't really interact with your own sisters. You're still a kid. You're scared.

Helen Wesley
Grade 9
Now resides in
Whitefish
Bay.

?

Helen Wesley
"She ran for Miss
Assiniboia, they told
her to keep running"

Gr. 9

Florence
Wood
Oxford
House
May 1964

Figure 24. Photo page from David Montana Wesley's scrapbook.

My sisters were older. But I was told that I couldn't interact with them—with the girls. That was pretty hard. You'd just wave, in the refectory, or during recess. That's the only time we were able to attempt some form of communication, just by waving. You couldn't talk.

We had rules here at the school, and we had to abide by the rules. If you were caught bypassing the imaginary line between the boys' and girls' sides of the playground, you would either go back to the dorm, or you were penalized in some other fashion. You wouldn't be able to partake in whatever was going to happen the following week, maybe. Like if there's an event, you can't go, because, "Sorry, you broke the rules, and you should have known. There's a line there." You may not see a line there, but it's there.

That's the way it was, a very hard moment in our lives to be separated from our own siblings.

What made it hard for me and my sisters was that we'd always lived in a little place called Longlac, but we'd never lived in the town. We always lived, like you say, "in the bush." Your friends are your siblings. We never lived on the reserve. We lived by two reserves. We were Cree from Fort Albany, and we lived by Ojibway people of that Nation. We're two different tribes. We were strangers in town from Longlac, Ontario. My parents didn't want us to live on the reserve anyway.

My father always believed that education was important for us so we could go further than them, because my parents didn't have education, but they wanted their children to succeed. We went to—as I recall, they were called Indian day schools back then—from grades one to eight.

They had rules too. They were Catholic, run by the Missionary Sisters of Christ the King. They were very rigid in their ideas about being a Catholic. They would always tell me that if I was not going to follow the Catholic religion and didn't start praying, that I was going to hell. Of course, you're taught early to believe that you're going to burn forever. You believe those things.

ASSINIBOIA RESIDENTIAL HIGH SCHOOL CADET
INSPECTION DAY - SPRING 1965
ASSIBOINE ARMY BARRACKS

HELEN WESLEY PTE. O. WESLEY AND
DOROTHY Wesley

Figure 25. Assiniboia Cadet Inspection Day.

Figure 26. Photo from David Montana Wesley's scrapbook.

I come from a family of sixteen. We all attended the Indian Day School, except maybe for the older ones who had already gone to other schools. They called them public schools.

It was an Indian Day School, so it was fast-forward through the curriculum. If you failed, you'd go right through—green light, and so on. The government had a program for us to keep coming, to continue to grade eight. After grade eight, you go to high school. It was hard for us to understand. Academically, it was hard for us because, like I said, there was fast-forward programming. You've got to keep up, even though you failed.

We were okay, even though it was hard for us to go to high school. And, coming back to Assiniboia, it seems like we were never out of the system they—the government—had. You had to follow all these rules and regulations. At first, it was hard for us. Me, anyway. Especially math, because I was in what they called commercial courses back then.

I wanted to be a draftsman. Mathematics was my problem. Indian Affairs—as they called it back then—said, "I don't think you can be a draftsman." They kind of dictated where I was going in life. "So, Dave Wesley, you're going to be an office worker." "Okay. What do I do?"

"So, Dave Wesley, I think you're going to be a bookkeeper." Of course, I didn't know what a bookkeeper was. I thought it was keeping books. It didn't say that it was accounting. "So, okay, I'll be a book-keeper." You know, I was fine with that, keeping books.

Well, now I'm a bookkeeper.

I was able to go to Assiniboia. Then, I went to regular high schools in Thunder Bay. But it was still a struggle. That's when I realized, I never heard the words "being bullied" back then, but you were just being beaten up all the time, because you were a Native person. I was one of the only Natives there, me and my other sister. It was back in the sixties, and we didn't have too many interactions with other Native people. They didn't have many schools there back then.

It was a hard time for me and my sisters to be successful in high school after Assiniboia.

Then we came back to Thunder Bay, and we were now starting in public schools. I went back home first. I took a bus. It was called the Canadian National Bus Lines.

Figure 27. Photo from David Montana Wesley's scrapbook.

I went to Port Arthur for school.[8] I went to Hammarskjold High School.

I'll always remember meeting my boarding family. This man, he was an older man. He was a scary man. He had a hunchback. He was waiting for me on the bus. He asked me, "Are you Dave Wesley?"

I looked at him and thought, "Who's this guy?"

"You come with me," is all he said.

Of course, I went right away.

He said, "You can stay at my place with me"—with him and his wife. They were my boarding parents.

I stayed there by myself, and there was another student. I thought that I was going back to hell, because his wife was vicious. She had rules. As soon as I got there—I'll always remember this: At supper-time, we were in our rooms upstairs. She called our names: "Dave and Harold, come on, let's go eat."

We were eating. She had two children of her own. I reached for something and she slapped me with her hand, and holy geez, after that I was afraid to eat because I didn't want to get whacked again. They always had special plates. "You don't eat lettuce. You eat something else." That was another thing I had to overcome, being ashamed to be part of the family.

After supper, she would say, "Go upstairs now. You don't come down."

I thought that was how we were supposed to live. Go upstairs and don't come down until suppertime. "What about going out?"

"No, you can't go out." Oh man.

I was in my room. "What about snacks?" "No, no snacks." I would get hungry. We had to—not steal—but try to get an extra snack somewhere. On weekends, we could go wherever we wanted to and come back for supper.

I had a friend who used to live there, and he helped us out with food.

I had the opportunity to call and get a message to my parents. We didn't have a phone. We were hungry. We didn't eat enough. My parents sent a box of food, like Klik, the canned food. I kept it in my room, underneath my bed, but I was caught by the mother, my boarding parent. She said, "What's this?"

"Oh, I don't know, it's food."

"How'd it get here?"

"My parents."

She took it away from me anyway. I couldn't eat it.

That was another struggle I had to fight with.

We had a school counsellor at Indian Affairs. He was pretty good. I told him what I was going through: "I feel like I'm not part of the family here. I can't eat after supper. I'm afraid to eat. I don't want to get strapped again."

He believed me when I told him, "I'm not getting enough food, like one sandwich for school lunch." There was an older man sitting at the table. We opened our little bags with one sandwich. He saw that, and he got up and said, "Hey, you come with me. We're moving you right now to another place."

I'll always remember him. He was a good man.

The next day we moved, but we didn't know where we were going to now.

But the family we moved in with were really good. They were an Italian family. They welcomed us into their home.

They had three kids who were just babies.

I ended up staying there for years.

Not for school. After high school, I went to college. I was becoming older now. Things were getting better, and I was happy there.

One day I said, "Well, I've got to go out. I'm older now. I've got to be on my own." I went to college and university and got my education.

If I could backtrack a little bit about when I was going through hard times with the high school curriculum. I quit school for one day. When I got home back in Longlac, my father looked and said, "Son, what are you doing here?"

"I had to quit. I'm having a hard time."

He was really disappointed. I knew he was disappointed, because he wanted us to learn how to pursue a good job.

He looked at me and said, "Well son, you can live here, but you can't eat here."

I said, "What? I'm going to starve."

And he said, "OK, well you go back to school then and you can go eat."

Later on, he said, "I want you to make sure to be educated and be able to get a job."

I always remembered what he said to me. I furthered my education. I went to college to get my business administration degree. That's how my career started, being an accountant. It was good. I enjoyed that part of my life. Things were getting better. I could get a job. I was getting paid. I was working. I was able to help my family, my parents. They were getting older, and it was my turn to make sure my parents had their needs met. It's a cycle. They raise you to be good person, but in my hard times—well, for all of us—we never forgot the way our parents raised us. They didn't want us to live in poverty the way

Figure 28. Photo from David Montana Wesley's scrapbook.

they lived back then. They wanted us to be educated so life would be good for us.

They teach you, you can understand what they say. You listen.

So that's a part of my life from being in the Indian day school to come here to residential school, and the experiences of Assiniboia.

But I wasn't aware of it being a residential school. I wasn't aware of the other students, that they went to residential schools earlier than my time. You never heard about the bad stories. You'd hear about how the government cheated the Native people. We were in prison more or less. All the hard times, how they affected our lives.

I heard it later on from my older sisters. They went to residential schools when they were younger, but they never said anything to us about their experiences at residential schools. They went to a school in the Kenora area, where there were residential schools.[9]

I didn't realize that my mother went to residential school.

My sister used to look after my mother when she was older. She used to cry all the time when she was older. She didn't want to be

Figure 29. Boys skating on an outdoor rink behind the McIntosh School, c. 1960–65.

bathed or to be showered, because she'd be crying. My sister asked, "Why are you crying? You never cried before."

I guess it reminded her of her residential school experience. She was actually scalded by the supervisors with hot water for punishment.

Holy, man, I wasn't aware of that. Then I became angry with myself.

You want to get even with whoever the perpetrators are, because they hurt your mom.

That's how I learned how residential schools were being operated. Even today, I hear a lot of stories, and I know how they feel.

That was my experience with residential schools and being out there, and the struggles we had as Native people to better ourselves. Sometimes you've got to fight. I was very passive. I was a very quiet guy. I'd get beaten up in high schools, you know. But I kept going, even though I was being mistreated. Because you always remember your parents: "You gotta go. You gotta keep going . . . no matter what."

So that's my experience in life through the high schools and Assiniboia.

Our School

Assiniboia, the first Indian Roman Catholic High School in Manitoba, opened its doors in September, 1958, with four teachers and one hundred students in the Grades 8, 9, and 10.

That same fall His Grace Archbishop Philip Pocock blessed the school and put it under the patronage of "Our Lady of the Holy Rosary".

After three years of operation the Grades IX- to XII are taught and the Grade Eight students remained in their respective schools. Since 1961, there have been a few graduates of whom Joe Guy Wood and Oliver Nelson were the first.

Assiniboia participates with her flying colors in various extra curricular activities such as Public Speaking, Football, Hockey, Red Cross, Army Cadets, and Community Welfare Planning Council.

Assiniboia had many distinguished visitors such as their Excellencies Bishop Paul Dumouchel O.M.I., Bishop Paul Piche O.M.I., and Miss Helen Fairclough when she was Minister of Immigration and Dickie Duff of the (Toronto Maple Leafs).

These are a few historical facts about Assiniboia High.

Figure 30. Page from the 1964 Assiniboia Yearbook.

Assiniboia High School All Indian Hockey Team 1960 won the Baldy Northcott Trophy, being champions of Junior B class of the Manitoba Amateur Hockey Association.
Front, from left: goalie Riley Runearth, coach Laurent Marchildon, captain Melville Courchene, Rev. Fr. O. Robidoux, O.M.I., principal, assistant coach Luc Marchildon, Collin Moar; middle row: Ralph Robinson, Harvey Nepinak, Oliver Nelson, Edward Papaunakes, Joe Guy Woods and Marcel Flett; back row: Paul Emile Wood, Paul Jobb, Bernard Linkalter, Gordon Nepinak and Isaias Bee.

Figure 31. Assiniboia Boys Hockey Team, 1960.

WHAT THE HELL AM I DOING HERE?

Hubert (Gilbert) Hart

Kinosawi Sipi – Norway House Cree Nation, Manitoba

Attended Assiniboia, 1964–68

Transcribed from an oral interview.

In 1964, I started at Assiniboia in grade nine. I remember it because I was in grade eight in 1963, and I remember the story about John F. Kennedy getting shot. I remember it clearly. The next year I came to Assiniboia.

I remember we came from Norway House by a plane and we landed at St. Andrews airport. They picked us up from there. We landed at night, and then we came here at night. We were all tired. We headed straight to where we were supposed to sleep.

The grade nines were put on the bottom floor. The dorm had two stories. When you were in grade nine and ten, you were on the first floor, and when you got to eleven and twelve, you were moved up.

We were stuck there. As we were walking in, the dorms were set up bunk bed–like, army style. I didn't know much about Assiniboia when I arrived the first night. We came in at night, so we just slept. We woke up in the morning, then went and had breakfast. And we saw all of these people all over the place. I'm wondering, "What the hell am I doing here?"

One thing about it, when I first came in here, I had my brothers and sisters in the school. It made it easier for me. That's one of the things that made it easier for me to attend Assiniboia, because several relatives from my mom's side were here. We started grade nine. Every morning we went to school in the building to the east of our dorms. That's where our classes were.

We studied more or less the same topics as everybody else, such as math and English. They assigned you any optional courses they had. They had typing, drafting, and other options. But then they put me in a French course. They put me in there and I didn't even understand. "What the hell?" I took it. I didn't like it.

By the end of the year, I failed grade nine because I failed French. I kind of thought about it, about the next year and going back. I thought, "What the hell am I going to do? I want to get back to Assiniboia." As they were loading up the plane to fly off, I snuck in. The guy writing names down asked me, "What's your name?"

"My name is Gilbert, Gilbert Sydney Hart."

He looked at me. "OK, where are you going?"

"Assiniboia Residential School."

Grounds and buildings of Assiniboia School, set in Winnipeg's residential area of River Heights.

Figure 32. Grounds and buildings of Assiniboia Indian Residential School, 1966.

I signed "Gilbert Sydney," and I did my grade ten.

By about the middle of Christmas, the guidance counsellor looked around and said, "Who the hell is this Gilbert?"

But I was passing my courses, so they let me stay in grade ten. I was taking typing as well. It was good. I got to Assiniboia in kind of a sneaky way, but it had to be done. It was fun. The five years I was there, I think were the best time of my life.

We had volleyball. In grades one to eight, we never had sports. It was all academic and stuff. We didn't have a gym and stuff like that, but then when I came here, all of a sudden, we had a gym. We could play volleyball and basketball. Of course, we played hockey all the time. We were not a very good team in volleyball and basketball. Other teams used to blow us away. They'd make us play the good teams here so we could get blown away. The first two years we got pretty used to it.

In grade ten and eleven, we were doing better. And, in hockey, the other city teams couldn't beat us.

They had a strict rule about sports. You had to have a certain grade percentage to play sports. That's what kept us motivated; we wanted to be on the sports team.

It was kind of fun. We played a lot of sports. They had a high fence. That big fence they had was about eight feet high all around. It was our boundary line. It is now a treeline—you could not go past it. It was the boundary line for the school. It was to keep us in our own place. If you wanted to meet the girls, you had another boundary line, an imaginary one—you were not allowed to pass it, the imaginary line. Everybody knew. You could stand on this side and the girls could stand on the other, and you could talk to each other. But there was no crossing. Because the rules were strict at that time and you had to follow them.

Everybody had their own area. It was hard to communicate. But as the years went on, I think in the sixties, between 1965 and 1966, we could mingle more with the girls. We could walk around here with them and stuff like that. Before that, forget about it. But then we had a change of staff, and they had different views of life at that time.

We used to go sit out on the hill over there and talk with the girls, and people walked by. Nobody cared. That's the way it was. We started mingling with each other. And what happened is we started mingling with each other and then started skipping class.

You know the reason. Assiniboia started losing people. Students started running away. These were young people at the age of fourteen, fifteen, sixteen, seventeen, and eighteen. They were at an age where rules seem to no longer apply to you anymore, like everything else.

That kind of changed. For people, it's their freedom. Now they had a freedom that they didn't know how to handle. When they didn't know how to handle their freedom, they just went ahead and did whatever they wanted. They had no parents. They became like their own boss. They could sneak away to town, go have a beer, come back drunk. Something like that. And in the sixties, everybody knows that at that time there were hippies, and that's the time they introduced all these drugs, marijuana, and stuff like that. Kids got caught up in all of it. A lot of them quit school, because they got caught up in this. They'd get kicked out of school, because they got drunk or they would get caught smoking up. So off they went. They didn't last that long.

But a lot of us didn't get caught. A lot us just stayed away from that. We went into town too, but we didn't get involved in all of that.

All the courses that were taken in grades nine, ten, eleven, and twelve were here, in this school. We had pretty good teachers and a few people nobody ever liked. With all the teachers in the world, it's always that way.

But that's the way it was. Our school life was a simple little thing. We'd get up in the morning, go have breakfast or we'd get the breakfast ready. We'd line up as usual at breakfast time. It was a good meal. I said that it was a better meal than at the other schools. And the food was good. I wouldn't complain about it.

The nun who was the first cook at the school is still alive. She was the cook there, and she's still around. She was twenty-one years old when she started working here. She was the cook, and she's still alive. Oh my God, I just saw her yesterday at the reunion. Last night I said, "It can't be. It can't be her."

She was a pretty good cook, put it that way. And she made sure everybody ate. That was her belief. If you have a good meal, you'll have a good life. You would then be able to study, and work, stuff like that. That's how she put it.

Besides the fact that the food was good, most of us never went home. We stayed Christmas, summer. I only went home one summer. In 1967, I finally went home for a while, maybe a month, and then I came back. I couldn't stand it.

Nineteen sixty-seven was the time of the Expo, and I went to Windsor, Ontario, for a student exchange that summer. I remember that. But my mom wanted me home, so I went home for a while. And then I took off.

Then they started this thing they call integration. They were working on that at about that time. They started bringing students from different schools into our school, asking them to come for the dances and stuff like that.

They brought some students from Kelvin High; I think they brought some students from there. So, the boys sat on this side, and of course the girls on the other side. And they were sitting on the other side before the dance started. They wanted to integrate everybody. They had to go and ask for somebody to dance when the music started. It was so funny. And, of course, this white girl comes along and walks up to me. My friends and I were sitting there saying, "I hope she doesn't ask us"—In our language—"to dance." She comes and stands in front of me.

"Do you want to dance?"

I looked at her, "Oh no, no no."

I was scared, eh?

I tried to waltz, but I was kind of stiff. Finally, she started talking. It was the first time I talked to a white girl. We used to see them around, but never talked to them.

We were dancing, and she said, "Relax for a while." It was the first time I ever danced. After that, she came and sat with us. We were sitting on a table. They came and sat with us, talking to us and asking about the school and everything. They started really relaxing. They became our friends, and we started talking with them. Then after a while, the boys were sitting on this side. They asked her, "What's your name?"

She said, "My name is Sydney."

And all the boys were laughing, eh?

The girl asked, "Why are you laughing?"

"His second name is Sydney." That is my name, eh?

Figure 33. Photo from David Montana Wesley's scrapbook.

We were laughing.

Later on in my life, when my daughter had a girl, I told my daughter that I wanted her to name her Sydney. Then I told her the story. She just laughed. That's my granddaughter's name, Sydney. She lives in Winnipeg.

I still remember her. It makes me feel good after all these years. It kind of changes your perspective. Meeting her made it easier for me to go to school away from Assiniboia, when they sent us to local high schools. When they wanted to send me to St. Boniface, it made it easier for me to talk to the other people.

I kind of enjoyed it when I went to St. Boniface. I made a lot of friends. I still remember a lot of them by their names. All of those guys—I still remember them. They became my friends out there and I can still remember them, because it was easy for me to move into the school. It was fun.

I think I learned a lot while at Assiniboia, because when I went to university, it made it easy for me to be in university. I could ask questions; I could do any little thing I wanted. That's what university's all about. If you can't study, you can't work, you can't ask questions.

It made my life a little easier—not that it was easy, because I got quite involved with alcohol too for a while there in my life, like everybody else. But I think for me, when I first came here, and by the time I left, I think it was a good experience, for me anyway. I don't have any regrets from it. The other people might have regrets, but I don't.

Everybody has their own experience. I had a good experience, and I don't regret that I came out here. I'm very happy that I came to meet a lot of these people here. They make me feel good. Another of my chapters is closed and we move on. They're talking about another reunion. So, who knows?

That's going to be a memory for me when I leave from here. When I drive home tomorrow after the reunion, I'll probably stop by and just say, "What the hell did I just do?" Because when I drove in after I left on Thursday, I didn't know what to expect.

I didn't become a teacher, but I was hired as an educational assistant in 1974 and I became part of the educational system when I returned home from Assiniboia. Then, all of a sudden, something opened up: I participated in an open university program where you work and go to school in the summer. In the spring and summer session you go to school.

It took me a long time, and then finally I graduated when I was an old guy—thirty-four years old, I graduated. And I worked there until I retired last year.

It was fun. It was a fun life. I taught a lot of outdoorsy stuff.

In two weeks' time, I'm going to start working with the Ministry, outdoorsy stuff. That's what I do. I love what I do. Schools fly me in to do presentations on residential school. I love doing it. It's fun. It's fun talking about it.

People talk about their own personal residential school experience. That's only my own personal experience. Nobody else has it. But only Assiniboia was a really good experience. They had a lot of things going on. I think they kept us doing a lot of stuff. We had cadets. In the summertime, we had that. Every week we had something to do. We had camping. We didn't get isolated. We had things to do outside.

We made money. Sometimes, we'd go clean up for these millionaires here, and rake leaves and stuff like that.

And then sometimes we'd go shovel snow from walks. When we had that big storm in 1966, one of the big, big blizzards we had, I made a lot of money on that thing.

I got brand new skates out of it, my own brand new skates. I made a lot of money. All of these people, they'd come walking past with their shovels and they'd call you, "Come on." I could pick up a lot of money because people wanted their walks shovelled. It was good.

That's how we made our own money.

Sometimes the farmers from out of town wanted somebody to help them with their potatoes or their harvest. They'd call the school, and we'd go. We'd make our money, and they'd feed us well. Oh, my God. I think I ate lots over there. Because when you eat, it's not a little plate; it's a big plate. Holy, man.

I think I had my fun years in here. I have no regrets. I got invited to a graduation for one of the girls in there. She's here, and she still remembers it. Forty-eight years ago, she said. That's the last time I'd seen her.

But that's part of how people remember. They remember the good times. They remember everything. For me, that was my good time.

KĒKWAN-OCHIY? WHY?

Betty Ross
Pimicikamāk Nīhithawī (Cross Lake, Manitoba)
Attended Assiniboia, 1962–63 and 1963–68

Tansi N'otemak,
Nanaskomon naspich, kiapich ekuskihtahyan eh achimostatakohk
kakispanihkowan niso residential schools kaki-puskīstaman
otēh pēwtanahk.

Greetings, all my relations. Today, I feel honoured to share with
you my journey and life experiences within the two residential
schools I attended from 1953 to 1968. Please remember that I will
need to pause every now and then for composure due to the fact that
it's very difficult to go back and revisit those eras today.

I attended Assiniboia Residential School at 621 Academy Road
in 1962 and 1963, then again in 1963 to 1968. It is also essential
to mention the fact that prior to Assiniboia Residential School, I
attended St. Joseph's Residential School from 1953 to 1956, and again
in 1962 and 1963, at Cross Lake, Manitoba, my original community.

Figure 34. Ecole Saint-Joseph de Cross Lake, c. 1905–45.

74

Please journey with me through my St. Joseph's Residential School years from 1953 to 1962. First, I need to mention the fact that I was abandoned by my biological mother at a very early age. If you ever come across my story, *Sugar Falls*, authored by David Robertson, launched in 2011, it's a must-read as it illustrates my early years and harsh experiences at St. Joseph's Residential School.

I was custom adopted by a childless couple. As I hold an eagle feather today, which represents Truth, I am reminded of the fact that I couldn't possibly have survived the past traumas of the residential school experiences of that era if my father, who custom adopted me, didn't take the time to teach me and plant the seeds of spiritual, cultural, and traditional values and belief systems within the recesses of my being.

Prior to entering St. Joseph's Residential School, we used to travel to Norway House by canoe to visit relatives, namely the McKays and Osborne families. To this day, I cherish the wonderful years I spent with my relative, Helen Betty Osborne, before her horrific tragedy in The Pas. We made awesome future plans. She wanted to be either a nurse or an educator. We shared hilarious secrets, boy crazy giggles and good laughs to the universe. I can still hear her mom calling us for supper in Cree, "Bechy-si-sak! Peymihtsok akwah," "Betties, come home for supper now." We used to just roar with laughter. Helen Betty Osborne rocked my world. I changed my name to Betty in 2000 to honour her spirit with the utmost respect. I need to pause now.

Upon our return to Cross Lake, one morning my father was sobbing at the foot of my bed. I asked him in Cree, "Kēkwan ēwchi mātohwon nipapa?"—"Why are you crying, Father?"

He responded in Cree, "Wuntipiskak kikahyan-mīna kakwatukītan mīchetoh Askih!"—"You will be in a dark place for many years where you will experience torture and trauma!"

I couldn't comprehend the meaning of his vision at that early age.

I enjoyed my carefree childhood, my home environment where I experienced strong family roots, love, and the traditional ways of life.

Since our house was right across the lake from St. Joseph's Residential School, I never looked at the school, even though I used to hear yells and shouts from the children at recess times. Instead, I found a sanctuary not far from our house. The surrounding shrubs and trees provided comfort and warm shelter. I was alone with my thoughts. I used to feel eerie as though something bad or sinister was about to happen. Whenever that feeling surfaced, I clutched both hands deep into the earth moss as if something was trying to pull me away from my comfort zone. This experience was ongoing, and little did I realize that my father's vision was inevitable.

Our door was always open for people to drop in for visits any time of the day, and one evening just after supper, a priest appeared at the doorway, approaching me. He pulled hard on my right wrist, stating "You come with me."

I screamed loud in fright as he pulled me out of the door, down to the bank and into a canoe. My mom and dad followed in horror. I reached and clenched my father's hand, shaking with fear, wondering and asking, "What's happening?"

He replied with grief, "Asa ispaniw ōma kakīhtitan, mino-iskwesiwiy, kawina sasīpītah"—"It's time. Be a good girl. Listen and obey." With tears in his eyes he stated, "Kawina wīkach wanikiskisiy kanachi-kiskinomakewina. Kitehihk kanawenihtah kakikē. Ekwanih-kēsapohtahikowan!"—"Never forget the sacred teachings I instilled in you. Honour them in your heart as they will help you to survive the systems."

Again, I couldn't really understand what he meant, being just a little girl at that time. This was the beginning of trauma after trauma in those dungeons. At St. Joseph's Residential School, the priests, nuns, and brothers basically tried to crucify me because of who I was. I experienced every kind of physical, emotional, mental, spiritual, verbal, and sexual abuse in that institution. They forced me to memorize Latin verses from the Bible—two straps for each mistake; and gave me tiny orange pills to take, where I lost consciousness every time, only to wake up naked, cold, and scared to death.

The nuns used either hot scalding water or ice-cold water, using hard bristled brushes to try to wash off my brown skin, to make it clean and white. Most nights, I used to sneak peeks through the window just to look at our house across the lake, shivering with the worst kind of lonely tears, silently.

I felt short-lived peace and the worst kind of homesickness. If I cried, never-ending straps continued. Even if I sat silently, I would get sharp, vicious straps for no apparent reasons.

One time, I uttered a Cree word softly to one of the girls, without knowing that a nun stood behind me. She heard what I said and immediately slammed my head on the cement floor, kicking my left ear with her pointed Oxford shoes. To this day, the hearing in my left ear is shattered. I also experience chronic migraines due to repeated head bangs on cement walls by nuns if I missed a marching step.

Every morning, we'd march toward the chapel before breakfast, and many of us fainted during long hours kneeling and praying due to hunger. There is so much more, but here I pause to take care of Betty.

Because my father instructed me to obey and listen to authorities, I never shared with my parents the horrific injustices I endured inside those merciless walls. Finally, in 1961–62, I was transferred to Assiniboia Residential School in Winnipeg, where I experienced deep-rooted culture shock. The environment felt so alien. I felt lost, lonely, confused, a total shattered wreck. I felt so bruised, damaged, and couldn't concentrate on my studies due to isolation. I cowered under authority figures, very passive, withdrawn, introverted, and so on.

Coming from such an abusive institution as St. Joseph's Residential School, I felt very cautious, vigilant and held onto trust issues that first year. The shame from St. Joseph's Residential School consumed and blinded my being from setting my spirit free as a fifteen-year-old teenager.

I totally missed out on so many privileges. Instead of moving forward, I felt backward and stuck. I came to Assiniboia Residential School wearing moccasins, which were thrown away; and I had to wear uncomfortable black-and-white Oxfords instead.

I felt awkward with my different wardrobe. I was afraid to make any mistakes, almost welcoming straps if I made the wrong moves or did things differently. I felt as though I was just an injured puppy that needed healing, but everybody was oblivious to my dilemma.

To my utter dismay, I failed my grade and I was sent back to St. Joseph's Residential School in 1962–63. At the Cross Lake school, the nuns made a mockery of my failure. In those days, there were no supports in place. The chronic abuse systems continued, but this time I took the initiative to go within the recesses of my being, not feeling any physical pain. Deep inside I heard and felt my father's teachings. I felt warm and safe where no one could every touch and hurt Betty ever again. I found a haven of inner strength, resilience, and joy of life deep within; and I was ready to fly south again.

Figure 35. A nun and another woman in the kitchen at Cross Lake Indian Residential School, Cross Lake, Manitoba, February 1940.

So, from 1963 to 1968, I was back at Assiniboia Residential School, armed with confidence and self-esteem, or so I thought. The abuse there was not too invasive, but was still there, only invisible. I just went with the flow, making real friends, speaking my language, and slowly joining social circles. I remained vigilant though, as I was just emerging from my safe cocoon. There were trust issues I couldn't handle. I didn't want a boyfriend even though I suffered several boy crushes to no avail. I totally stayed away from the dating scene at seventeen years old.

I remember being a follower, a wallflower during dance socials, and being so self-conscious. It was a roller-coaster ride, and I tried hard to fit in. Here, I was so influenced by the nuns' piety and used to join them in their afternoon reflections, because my shattered spirit needed spiritual food and comfort.

I remember Assiniboia Residential School as a hub of constant activity. Students remained busy with extracurricular activities such as hockey, football, curling, carnivals, army cadets, cheerleading, skating demonstrations, and so forth.

I settled down pretty much in my second year at Assiniboia Residential School, even though there were hurdles and challenges to overcome. I remember occasional outings to Camp Morton. Each year, my studies improved. I joined choirs, cheerleading, and skating sessions. In a way, I was part of the human race again. Rules and regulations were flexible, but structured. The teachers, supervisors, and staff were accommodating, friendly, and supportive. Some students never returned home from holidays, for whatever reasons.

I remember the highlights—whenever our boys brought back hockey and football trophies as champions. We felt Native pride right there within our own circle of successes. Our student council published a first edition of Keewatin yearbook, a lasting souvenir of Assiniboia Residential School.

Assiniboia Residential School taught us a legacy of the learning curve of education away from our communities and families. Most of us strived to be physically, psychologically, and mentally fit, to be eager, and willing to succeed. Once upon a time, a long, long time ago, Assiniboia Residential School was our haven away from our grassroots communities. Our families made huge, courageous sacrifices to let us go from their hearts in order to see us fly toward newer heights.

Some of us persevered, others waved goodbye, still others simply walked away and never looked back.

The residential school system either made you, or broke you.

In my last year of high school, I boarded at Assiniboia Residential School and attended Sacred Heart Convent, an all-white girl's school in Charleswood.

Something happened to my world at this time. I began to sneak out of Assiniboia at nights to attend some dances on Princess Street. I did this several times, until I was caught one night and punished with no black-and-white television privileges for months!

Once again, the fears of being left out in the cold returned. Even though I was dying inside for "freedom," I felt petrified of the looming world. What do I do? Where do I go? I never learned any life skills on how to face the outside world alone. Suddenly, I was bombarded with a gazillion questions. What will happen to me? There was absolutely no one to whom I could turn! I don't even remember if there were any guidance counsellors at Assiniboia or at the Convent, for that matter.

Going back a few years, when I was still cocooned inside Assiniboia, I was privileged to earn some babysitting jobs on weekends, always to the envy of some girls who labelled me as "Sister's pet"! I remember a time when a friend and I were chosen to work for millionaires (the Parkhill family) at their cabin on Lake of the Woods. I remember meeting Bob Hope there once and cooking his meal. My friend and I were so nervous to serve a celebrity that we accidentally burned his pie pitch black! What an embarrassment!

I remember Mr. Parkhill being over-protective of us. He used to pay us five dollars a week and we thought we were rich!

Back to my time at Sacred Heart Convent, there are some things I remember vividly. There was a chemistry teacher called Mr. Richards and us girls used to call him "To Sir with Love" since he looked so much like Sidney Poitier. He used to address me as "Lady Jane." One time in class he stated, "If you don't understand anything about chemistry, Lady Jane, axe me, Lady Jane, axe me!" We used to just holler with laughter!

At the Sacred Heart Convent School, we were all dressed in brown attire: brown Oxfords, pleated skirts, tunics, neck ties, with beige shirts. People used to ask if we sold cookies!

Many of my residential school colleagues are gone. My heart will always ache for them. Only a few of us residential school Survivors remain to this day and were strong enough to voice out, "This was not right." Today, as I close my eyes and reminisce, I see the halls, dorms, shower stalls, metal beds, cement floors, pictureless walls, lockers, mirrors, girls jiving to young love, loud radios, black-and-white TVs, sister in charge delegating chores, the girls' supervisor reporting to work inebriated, girls asking for cigarette puffs, ironing boards, daily recitations of "Hail Mary" and "Glory Be," girls borrowing clothes for special occasions, lining up for meals, boys and girls flirting, my secret crushes holding hands with new girlfriends, and I'm feeling ill with stomach butterflies. This is only a small fraction of an Assiniboia Residential School flashback.

There were ten of us girls attending the Sacred Heart Convent School while boarding at Assiniboia and only four of us graduated in 1968–69.

In conclusion, I am asking some hard questions. *Why!?*

Why residential schools?

Why couldn't they just leave us alone?

Did the government and churches achieve their goals?

What kind of mindset was in operation during that era?

Why this invasion of insidious actions of the worst kind?

Why did these two atrocious systems try to *crucify* me for *who* I *was*?

I have a million, gazillion "Whys" that will never be answered in this lifetime and beyond.

I'm seventy-three years old. KēKwan-Ochiy?

Why?!?

WE WERE TOLD TO HAND THE FLAME
TO A WHITE RUNNER

Charlie Nelson

Okwewanashko-ziibiing – Roseau River First Nation, Manitoba
Attended Assiniboia, 1964–69

Transcribed from an oral interview.

The first three years I was in residence and attended classes at Assiniboia. I mostly remember the third floor, the highest floor. There was the basement and then the first one and then the second one, and then there was the highest one.

My stay here was not that bad, because I was not too far away from home, and my dad would pick me up nearly every other weekend. He had a nice truck, so in an hour and ten minutes I was home.

Still, I was only in grade nine when I came to residential school. I went from grade one to six on the reserve, and then for grades seven and eight I went to the town school. It wasn't too bad. I was fourteen years old, leaving home in grade nine. In 1964, I might have been fifteen already.

The following summer I went to army cadets in Vernon, BC. I went for seven weeks. We would fly in on a four-engine propeller plane.

It was nice to go to BC in the summertime. They had lots of apples and stuff like that. You could go swimming. We ran track and field. My time was 4:40 for a mile; that's what I ran. I thought I'd tied this big, tall guy, but no. That's a little bit of my track and field history.

We used to have track and field at Assiniboia. Once in a while, we'd go run. I'd follow some of the better runners. They would run from here up to the Perimeter. They'd go down by Roblin Boulevard. It was a pretty long run.

They asked me to run in the Pan-American games—the torch run—in 1967.

There were three of us from Assiniboia: Bill Chippeway, William Merasty, and me. I got to meet nine others. One of my friends was Russell Abraham; he's passed away now. There was John Nazzie. He's passed away too. There was another guy, Milton Mallett. He was a pretty good runner. I saw him in track and field one time in Sargent Park. He was pretty good.

We had Charles Bittern from Poplar River, who went to Birtle Residential School. He used to run; his story was told in the documentary about the Front Runners, the young Indigenous runners, including myself, who carried the torch for the Pan-Am games but were not allowed to bring it into the stadium.[10]

Figure 36. Aboriginal teenagers brought the Pan-American Games torch from St. Paul, Minnesota, to Winnipeg, only to have a white athlete take the glory lap in 1967.

And then there was Fred Harper from Red Sucker, I think, in the Island Lake area there. There was Pat Bruyere and Dave Courchene Jr. from Sagkeeng. I think that's about it, all ten of them.

It was nice. We travelled in two convertibles. One of them was a station wagon. We drove down and then ran from St. Paul, Minnesota, to the stadium. That's 500 miles.

We ran about anywhere from sixty to eighty miles a day—at that time we used miles. We ran in the summertime. They gave us some salt pills and stuff like that to make sure we didn't dehydrate. When you perspire, it removes some things from inside of your body, like the salts. They gave us that, and we had lots of Adidas products. We had Adidas shorts. That's what they gave us to run in.

They took some pictures here at the stadium of the ten of us. They lined us up and took a picture of us on the path up to where the flame would have been at the stadium. Then we went to the States. It was nice. Wherever we stayed, we stayed in hotels with air conditioning. It was the middle of summer. It was July and it was hot.

The previous Pan-American games were in São Paulo, Brazil. Because St. Paul is almost the same name, it represented that run. So, they got the flame from over there to come to St. Paul, and then we would bring the flame to Winnipeg to light the flame.

At the towns where we stopped, the city councils hosted meals and we would be given the opportunity to share some words. I didn't have many words to say at that time about who we were. We knew how to run, that's all.

Some of our families have a long history of running. My grandpa, whose name was also Charlie Nelson, was said to be always leading the runners. The one who told me the story—Clarence Henry—said that I wasn't far behind, remembering "Your grandpa was a good runner, a great runner."

There are stories about hunting a long time ago. We used to run after the deer. The deer is fast for a good little while, but you keep going. You run and be determined and keep running, and you'll catch up to him, because the deer gets tired after a while. These are some of the stories that I shared.

We brought the flame to the stadium. The people told us that 34 million people were going to be watching.

I was pretty nervous at the beginning in the stadium. We were told to hand the flame to this white runner who was famous. He was a white runner, and he ran the flame into the stadium. I didn't think too much of it myself at that time, but people said that they should have given us more exposure, to have run the flame that far.

We ran into the stadium behind that runner, but six of our runners were carrying the Pan-American flag. That was quite a thing to be asked to bring in the Pan-American flag. It's a big flag.

It was raining and there were puddles of water, so you had to kind of watch where you ran.

And I wanted to see Prince Philip in the stands, but I was looking down because I didn't want to stand in the water. So I didn't see him.

Thirty-two years later, they called us back to finish the journey. They wheeled us in on big canoes. The canoes might have been about twenty feet long. They had a little prop so we could put our hands on the handles there so we wouldn't fall down. These canoes had wheels on the bottom, and they had some runners who pushed the canoe. We were just waving and stuff like that.

Then we brought in the flame. Dave Courchene won the draw to be the runner to carry the flame in. Then he handed that flame over to a First Nations girl, Ida Whitford. She picked up the torch and started running. But right at the time when the torch was being handed, the wind came in and all the streamers and flags went horizontal, because of the wind, eh?

It was a big thing for us to feel, all of that. It was something spiritual for us to be part of that.

As a result of being on the Front Runners, I travelled. And I am still travelling. I'm going to the North American Indigenous Games next month [in 2017].[11]

Last year, we went to the Pan-American Games in Toronto. We visited the flame. We met the Premier.

This lady wrote a story about us in 1999. Thirty-two years later, she came and visited us in our homes, and she started to write about our experience.

One of the experiences of residential school is the runners having to run after runaway girls. One of them was called Rose. When the runner brought Rose back to the school, she got punished. They used a hockey stick on her and physically abused her. And that guy thought she had died.

Rose didn't die, and, in the film about the Front Runners, Rose was brought to see the runner who brought her back. "You're Rose," he said, "I thought you'd died." That's what he said to her. "I heard all that screaming, and now you're still alive and you're still encouraging us to run." He got Charlie Bittern to take up a cause for running and helping kids to do track and field.

I've been to quite a few places: Montreal, all around Toronto. We went to see the play and the film about our run. So we went to quite a few places: Southhampton, Ontario, and Wiarton, where that ground-hog is. It's south of Manitoulin Island. You cross the bridge and then you go down by Tobermory. We went all around there.

I went to Scandinavia twice. Denmark, Stockholm, Oslo. We went to northern Norway and north of Stockholm on the first trip. We visited the Sami people. Our experience: We had a chance to share some words about First Nations people. At least they can put a face to who are the First Nations people of Canada.

So that's a little bit about my experience with running.

We're going back to Toronto next month on the fourteenth [14 July 2017] to the North American Indigenous Games (NAIG). I have some grandkids who are going to participate in NAIG Games in basketball. And I think one of them might be in baseball. I think that's what it is. There are three of them.

I have a nephew who ran the Manitoba Marathon. It was twenty-six miles and there are about 600 runners. That's about two weeks ago.

Two years ago, he finished twenty-sixth. This year he finished about sixtieth, he said.

I think he might be thirty-four now. I'm not too sure, but he does look like a runner. He's six feet tall and lean. It's nice to see what he does. Maybe he'll still run.

I didn't see any physical abuse or sexual abuse. That's all I think about. I just say thank you. At the age of fifteen, it was time to get away from home, I guess.

Grade nine, ten, eleven, and twelve were here, and then I went to Kelvin High School for half a year and then half a year in Tech Voc [Technical Vocational High School, Winnipeg].

PART II
THE HOSTEL YEARS, 1967–73

Figure 37. Assiniboia playing fields viewed from Wellington Crescent.

At the start of the 1967–68 school year, Assiniboia was converted into a hostel for students attending Winnipeg high schools. The experiences of students during this time combine both life in the dormitories and study space (in the classrooms building) but also adjustment to integration into schools primarily populated by non-Indigenous students. They made new friendships at Winnipeg high schools, but also experienced racism and alienation. Just as once the government experimented with assimilative residential schools, now "integration" was the new experiment, and the students at Assiniboia were required to show determination and resilience as they ventured out from the Assiniboia campus more frequently, and without staff accompaniment.

It should be noted that some of the Survivors featured in the previous section continued at Assiniboia while it was a hostel, as is apparent in their remembrances. In this section, we feature two further Survivors, whose experiences occurred primarily within the hostel period. Further work is still to be done to connect with more Survivors from this era of Assiniboia.

YOU'RE NOT PROTECTING US

Carole Starr

Waanibiigaaw – Hollow Water, Manitoba

Attended Assiniboia, 1969–70

Transcribed from an oral interview.

I attended for six months. The reason they sent me here was because they didn't have high school in my community.

When I first got here, it was something new, something exciting. I was never really away from my family. It was my first time. I got to write letters every second day to my mom, and she wrote back.

I got lonesome. I had family here that attended, but I couldn't see my cousin, because he was on the boys' side, and we only saw each other at meals. We couldn't really talk, so we'd just wave at each other. There were days when I needed more than just a wave but we couldn't have that. It was difficult because we were almost close enough to touch, but it was not allowed.

I have a recurring dream: I'm leaving the residence, I get to the door, and the floor falls away. The door is there, but the floor is falling away, and I'm falling into darkness. I try to go back on the steps, and they're falling apart. And I wake up scared. I don't know why. I don't recall anything really bad happening to me.

Figure 38. Assiniboia classrooms building stairwell, 2017.

At the reunion yesterday, when I visited the old study hall, going upstairs was okay, because I remember just studying there. And I remember feeling so frustrated with French. I was okay with Latin. Latin was easy. But French, for some reason, I struggled with it.

Then our tour guide took us down to the basement, and right away my stomach started turning, my legs started feeling weak, and I started feeling heaviness on my chest. I was trying to breathe through that. There was this other guy talking. He was there years earlier than I was, so for him, that was the school. For me, it was the study hall. And I didn't know that. I didn't know it was classrooms, actual classrooms. It was interesting to hear from other students who were here before me.

Then it was my turn, and I started remembering that's the room in the basement. I was there for six hours, and I started to say that, and I couldn't talk anymore.

I looked down and felt "I got to get outta here." I couldn't breathe. And now I feel like I need to talk about that. But I don't know what it is that I have to talk about. I just didn't like being in there. I had to get out of there. It was heavy. I still feel it today.

All these years I said nothing happened to me. The reason I came to the reunion was because of my dreams. I said, "I need closure," but a closure to what? I don't know.

I've been thinking, "Was I abused?"

I have no memory of it. I don't even recall the supervisors, for some reason—the women. I don't recall their names.

I recall a Cardinal, but then I found out today it was John Cardinal, and he was a supervisor for the boys. There was another supervisor, who, for some reason, I don't know why, I can't remember him. The nuns, I also do not remember the nuns, but I know I didn't get along with them.

There was one, I don't even remember her name. Every Sunday, there was this Johnny Cash show on TV. There were quite a few of us who wanted to watch that, but it was getting past our curfew, our bedtime. And we would ask: "He's just going to sing one more song?"

And she would just say, "No, you go to bed!"

And then I asked the nun, "Don't you work for God? Don't priests and nuns work for God?"

She said, "Yeah."

"Well, isn't God love?"

"Yeah."

"So where's yours?" I said, "I don't see it in you."

And then she just told me to go, go to my bed. After that she kind of treated me differently from the rest. She wasn't outright mean, but she treated me differently because I asked her that question.

My experience with nuns before residential school was positive, it was nice. They were very kind, loving, and supportive. I don't recall having any contact with the priests. But the nuns, they did catechism with us and it was always stories and songs. However, we couldn't speak our language—the nuns did not allow this.

We grew up knowing not to speak our language in front of white people. And we always checked first to see if anybody was around and then we'd speak our language.

We were not allowed to speak Ojibwe here. We couldn't; we used to go by the bridge or under the bridge; there we could talk all we wanted.

It took me a while to finish my high school. I would get so close to graduating, and then I would sabotage everything. It took me years to get right through.

The work was okay. I just didn't want to finish it. I don't know if I was punishing myself for leaving. I left because there were new students in residence here, and they were very aggressive students. That was my first experience with sniffing glue and whatever. I don't know what else they used and I don't know how the boys managed to get onto the girls' side; but they were with girls from their community. There were three boys and girls who grabbed me, and they held the cloth with the glue, I guess—I don't know—over my mouth and nose. I had to breathe that in. I started kicking and trying to pull away;

and they finally let me go. I went to the supervisor right away and I told her. She said, "Okay." That was it.

To my mind, nothing was done, because the girls came after me for telling.

And I got mad. I was so angry. I went to that supervisor.

"You guys are not doing anything. You're not protecting us. I'm leaving. That's it. I'm not coming back."

And, I left. I had a cousin—he was a man at the time, and I knew he was going back home. I said, "I want a ride. Can you give me a ride?"

"Yep."

He gave me an address where he would pick me up after work, and I went there by bus. That was my very first time going on McPhillips Street. I never even knew there was a McPhillips Street.

And that was it. I went home to Hollow Water.

I wasn't going back, and nobody was going to make me go back. I did not feel safe there.

I had felt safe enough, but after those two incidents I didn't feel safe, so that was it. And that's the only memory I have of not feeling safe.

Otherwise, it was pretty good—the experience—staying there, getting to know students from other places. I thought it was wonderful that I got to hear other languages—like the Cree, and hey, I could understand their words; and the Swampy Cree, those I could understand clearly.

I thought that was amazing.

While hostelling at Assiniboia, I went to an all-girls school called Convent of Sacred Heart. It was past the zoo. The building's gone, apparently. I've never gone back.

I got to see the buffalo in the zoo every morning, and pass by the buffalo every day.

We used to save our bus tickets on Fridays, because we wanted to go downtown on the weekend.

This one day, there was a group of us. There must have been, like, six of us. We would walk through the park—through the zoo and Assiniboine Park. We walked through, along the river, to come down to the residence. I noticed this man; we kept meeting him. I found that weird; I thought it can't be a coincidence. Like, there can't be another man dressed the same way and look exactly alike. I started looking around. I was starting to feel nervous.

Then I looked to one side and there was a clearing there, another path off our path. And there he was, standing with his pants down.

I said, "Run." First, I said it in my language, and then I said it in English. There were six of us; I think there were like three of us who actually saw the weird guy expose his private parts to us. The other ones didn't see him. They didn't know why we were running, but they just ran with us.

That was the last time I walked that way. I wasn't going to go back. I didn't want to have that kind of experience again.

There was a Royal Bank across the street. I figured, "Well, I need bus money"—you know, to buy tickets—and, "I want to go down-town," to a movie or something. I needed money. So, I started walking around Academy Road here. I walked into the bank and I talked to one of the tellers, and I said, "I need a dollar, because I want to get money for the bus so I can go downtown and buy something."

She said, "Okay, we'll give you a job."

"Okay, well, what can I do?" I said.

And she said, "Well, you can clean up. Pick up our garbage and sweep up."

"Fine, I know how do to that."

I got my first money. In those days, I was fifteen. Children were allowed to go to the store and buy cigarettes. So, I did. I wanted to be a big person with money, so I bought cigarettes. Oh, my gosh, I had a lot of friends.

Then I noticed my cigarettes were going fast. I figured, "I've got to do something. Without being rude, without saying no." I didn't want to say no. I didn't want to be rude, so I switched brands to Camel menthol.

Without saying no, I said no. I started smoking menthol. Nobody liked those. And I still had my friends.

On weekends we had dances in the gym.

I was the shortest girl and there was this young boy from Shamattawa. I don't even remember his name but he was very tall. There was this event they did every fall and they had a queen and a king. The students were given tasks, pretty crazy tasks, to do. Some of them I remember; they had to use a ruler to measure the gym!

Some of them were sent to graves to pick pebbles from a certain grave. They were given a name, and then they would have to find that headstone and then collect pebbles or something. Some were told to dress up as a hockey player and go on a bus ride, the whole way around. Crazy stuff like that. They made me the queen. I didn't have to do anything. But I had to stand beside this tall, tall guy! And then I found out after why they made me queen. It was because I was the shortest and he was the tallest. We had to open the dance. Oh. Everybody else was laughing at us. As long as I didn't have to do any of that crazy stuff, I figured, if this is all I have to do, then fine.

I liked it at the Convent of Sacred Heart school. I didn't like the uniform, the brown uniform. You know those blazers and skirts, the Oxford shoes, and the yellow tie. We used to have a fashion show of our slips. We'd stand on a chair and say, "Okay, what does your slip look like?" Our clothes were all the same. The only thing different was our slips.

There was one girl—I'm bad with names, I can't remember—her parents had a horse ranch. Some weekends she would invite a few of the girls from the school, and we would go horseback riding. I enjoyed it. There were some good times.

Some of the meals were pretty okay. But, I remember every Thursday. I just dreaded Thursdays. After I got to know the menu, I didn't like Thursdays, because the main meat in there was garlicky and leftover from the week before. It tasted horrible.

To this day, I don't really care for garlic; except when I'm camping. We roast it over an open fire. There's an island and it's called Black Island. Every summer almost the whole community moves there. This started about twenty-five years ago. When I was a kid, my parents used to take us camping there. We still go to the same camp. I take my grandkids there today, where my parents took us camping.

* * *

There was this girl, Bella. She had a boyfriend. His name was Wilson something, and they broke up. So, she was under the blankets crying, "Oh this, and oh this."

And we were all trying to sleep.

I think there were fifteen of us in one dorm. And we had little cots, really small. These two girls were going to go and beat up Bella to try to shut her up. My friend Martina jumped up. "Don't you touch her; I'm not going to let you bother her," she said in Bella's defence. One girl jumped up. She was going to fight Bella but Bella didn't even know what was going on. She was too busy crying over Wilson, under her blanket.

Martina and this other girl started fighting, and another girl jumped in, she said "I'm going to fight Martina, too." Martina is my friend, so I also jumped in.

I said, "Don't bother her. Let them fight. If you jump in now, you fight me."

I didn't know if she was going to beat me up or not. I'm not a big fighter. I'm not a fighter. She was tall!

So, she moved closer to me and I stepped closer to her. Martina and the other girl were fighting away. Then the supervisor came in. I guess somebody went running for her. She got after us and told us to go to bed, to stop the fight. We did.

Bella was still laying in her bed, crying over Wilson. She had no idea what was going on.

I always used to hear my aunty. She went to the Sagkeeng Residential School,[1] and she said, "I was just a number there." I never understood her comment until I got here. I had a number, too—my bed and my locker were the same number.

There was a routine. That I remember. I'd get back from school, and I wanted to go and have a shower, and I couldn't find my undies. I didn't have any. But all our clothes are marked with a number. I told my supervisor, "I can't find any of my undies."

"Are you sure? Did you check the laundry basket?"

"Yes," I said. "I checked, it's empty."

The laundry was the day before, so I should have them. My clothes were there, except for my undies.

"Well," she said, "at supper time when everybody's out, get somebody to help you. Check the lockers."

I said, "Okay." So I asked Martina to help me.

Nobody was in our dorm, but they had all their own clothes. So, I went over to the next dorm and I found my undies. They were in the locker of this huge, big girl.

I said, "What? Why would she take mine? I'm the smallest here, and she's the biggest."

I took my undies all back and I went and put them in my locker. And I waited. After supper, I went up to the big girl. I told her, "I took back my undies. Don't you ever touch my stuff again."

And I was looking at her straight in the face, and pointing to her, and she was just backing away from me.

These are some of my experiences at Assiniboia.

I STUCK WITH IT

Martina Fisher (née Young)
Misko-ziibiing – Bloodvein First Nation, Manitoba
Attended Assiniboia, 1969–72

Transcribed from an oral interview.

I left home on a float plane. We landed in Pine Falls. Then we had to take a bus from Pine Falls to Winnipeg. It was my first time on the bus. I was on a plane once before. I saw Winnipeg for the first time when I was twelve.

And then, coming to the residential school here, I was the only Anishinaabe the first year I was here. I was the only Saulteaux (Anishinaabe), and when I first got in there, there were four girls from up north; they were Cree. The first thing they told me was that because I was Saulteaux and they were all Cree, I wasn't going to last for the whole year. As soon as they said that, I said, "I am going to stay." Their taunts convinced me to stay for that full year. I stayed even though they were trying to intimidate me many times, and trying to scare me away. I stuck with it.

At one point, I accidentally broke a window because I got angry. For some reason, I didn't get in trouble.

But the thing I remember is that I was the only one from my family at Assiniboia. I had a cousin on the boys' side. He's passed on now, but he was my cousin. As soon as we got in there, we weren't allowed to have contact. We grew up together. He was like my brother, but we couldn't have contact when we ate. We ate separately. The girls on one side, the boys on the other side.

Every morning we stood in assembly lines to do chores.

I sometimes worked in the kitchen. I buttered lots of bread, lots of toast, or we would help serve.

We didn't go to school here, but apparently somebody said that the old school was our study hall. For some reason, I blocked that out. I blocked it out, but when I went there yesterday, I almost fell to my knees. I almost fell, because for some reason in one of those rooms, I went limp. I don't know why. But I could feel energy, and it was a heavy, heavy energy that I felt in there.

So, I don't know what happened. I don't know if I blocked some stuff when I was in the residential school.

A lot of residential school Survivors remember their numbers. We all had a number. I don't know what my number was, but my number was on all my clothes and the bed that I slept in, but I don't know what it was.

Figure 39. Assiniboia Indian Residential School classrooms building, c. 1963–65.

And we all had to stand in line again to have a shower. They had open showers for us to shower. We were very embarrassed a lot of times.

Coming from the north, we mainly wore long dresses in our tradition. When I came to school here, our dresses were very short.

And then we had to go to church like that. It was very uncomfortable, very uncomfortable, because I felt dirty. I felt like I was showing too much of my body.

So those were times I remember that I felt it wasn't right.

Coming to the residential school, the first thing that the students warned me about was not to go in the priest's office alone. I didn't know what they meant by that, but I was careful that every time I had to go to the office, I had somebody with me just to protect myself, you know?

I tried not to get in trouble. Because of the things I was hearing, I had to protect myself, to some degree anyway.

But it was so lonely because, as I told them in there, there was no communication with my mom and dad, and my siblings when I left. There was no such thing as a phone. So once in a while I would write a letter to my mom. I don't remember ever receiving a letter back, a reply from her.

And, so, that's how it was. We were always lonesome. We took others as our sisters, our brothers, but mainly our sisters.

The only time we had a good time was when—I don't know how often, maybe once a month or maybe less than that—we would have a dance in the gym. There we would be together with the boys and have fun and dance, but, other than that, we all had to stay separate.

The thing is that my mother went to a residential school, and the way she parented me was corporal punishment. And, so, I did that to my own children—the first three of my oldest children. Until today, I'm paying for it, because my mom's gone. I never ever got angry at my mom, because I thought that was normal. But to my children, it wasn't normal. They knew already that was abuse, and so, now I'm paying for it because they show it when they get angry with me. And I have to live with that, you know? I can't even say that I'm sorry, because the damage is already done. I didn't know how to parent. When my children were maybe up to five or six years old, I would hold them and say "I love you," but after that I couldn't, because my mom couldn't say "I love you" to me.

I had nine children, and I've lost four already. The first one I lost was a SIDS; he died in his sleep. And I was so angry at God.

And the second one I lost, he was murdered. He had a knife through his heart.

And the last two I lost within the last four or five years. Four or five years ago, I lost a daughter. She was sixteen. Before she died, she was the one who taught me how to say "I love you." She said "Mom, say 'I love you.'" I couldn't say it for a long time. She said, "Mom, look at me. Say 'I love you,'" until I could say it. My daughter taught me how to say "I love you."

But when she was twelve years old, my daughter said, "Mom, I'm going to leave when I'm sixteen."

I said, "Don't talk like that, Alexis."

"Mom, I know I'm going to leave when I'm sixteen."

I don't know how she knew. And when she was sixteen years old, she would always call me—we lived in Winnipeg. She was going to school at Gordon Bell.

Three, four, or five times a day she would call me. She would always let me know where she was. She would call me, "Mom, come and get me." No matter where she was, no matter what time it was, I went and got my daughter.

And one day, when she was sixteen, at midnight I saw her. She said, "Mom, I'm going to go have a smoke outside."

"Well, come back right away," I told her. And she never came back. And then the next day, she never called. And then I told my sister, "Virginia, Alexis never called today. She always told me where she was. I think there's something wrong."

The next day again, nothing.

On my phone, I still have my message that says, "Alexis, please phone home." I wrote down that last message.

And then the second day when she didn't come home, I went to the police station by myself, alone. I walked in. There was a lady behind the reception, and there were two cops behind the counter. I went straight to the cops, because I wanted to report that my daughter was missing. I went to those two cops—one was younger, one was older—and the older man said, "How can I help you?"

I said, "I came here to report that my daughter is missing."

And the other one started chuckling and laughing and saying, "Well, your daughter might show up. You know about girls."

I looked at him and I said, "It is not funny. This is not a funny matter." I raised my voice and it went quiet in there. I said, "You don't treat me like that. I'm here to report my daughter."

And then the other one cut in, and he said, "I'll help you." He said, "I'll give you this number; you call missing persons."

So that's what I did.

She went missing on Sunday. Sunday night she left, then Monday. Tuesday, I reported, and they started investigating. And they started calling me. Thursday, they finally said, "This is your daughter. We want you to come and—how do you say that—identify her." And I did. But she was the one who taught me to say "I love you."

And my son, I lost him a little over a year ago at thirty-five. He committed suicide.

And you know, these are the things that they're talking about, the intergenerational effects of Indian residential schools. Because I didn't know how to parent, and I didn't know how to deal with certain stuff with my children. Even though I told them after a while that I loved them, I couldn't keep them. I couldn't go to them.

And these are the things that I have to suffer every day. And especially my sister, she was a couple of years older than me. She went to a residential school. We buried her when all this came about, because she didn't know how to deal with it. My sister went to prove to herself and everybody that she could do a lot more than what we were told. She became a professor and she worked at the University of Winnipeg for many years. She's helped all nationalities of students, encouraging them. But when the Indian residential schools issue came up, she couldn't get out of that anger. For the first time, it just opened something that she'd shut. And she never drank in her life. She drank herself to death. I knew she was doing that and I couldn't stop her.

These are the things that are happening that we have to deal with day in and day out in our homes, in our community, and in ourselves—within myself too. I thought, "I've done a lot of healing. I healed enough." No, no. Something keeps coming up almost every day. Almost every day, something will trigger, "No, you're not okay. You're just strong. You're just patient."

And if it wasn't for our spiritual belief and trust in a higher power, we would never survive, but we survive because of that. And I believe that I know that my children are looking after me, because they're in a good place. I have to tell that to myself every day, that my children are in a good place, that they're okay, that they're being looked after; and I'm here only for a while, to see them again.

These are the things that we deal with.

I went to Neechi Commons on Main Street with my friends to eat, and there was a mother and daughter at the next table. The mother was trying to talk to her daughter, and the daughter said to her mom, "Where were you when I was growing up?" That's what we hear: "Where were you?" is what my kids tell me. And, yet, I went to work as a single parent—most of my life, a single parent—to take care of my children. But they still thought—to them, because I was away from home—that I neglected them, that I wasn't there for them. And that hurts.

But, all in all, it's hard with our families apart. My mother was a residential school Survivor. Later on, she talked to me. She said, "Martina, you're going to learn lots. Take what you can, what you need, and leave the rest." That was a good teaching of my mom.

She sang in church, and my dad played the organ. They looked after the church all those years that they were living.

My mom said, "Martina, there is no hell." That really, really helped me lots when she said that there is no hell. Everybody, we're suffering here. We suffer here. "This is hell—on earth," she said, eh? "When we die, we go to a good place." And that was encouraging for me, for my mom to tell me that, because when I was growing up in church and in school back home, they taught us to believe that we were going to hell.

I was so scared, I was just shaking when I went to my first sweat lodge, and my late sister who had cancer at that time said, "No, no, no, come inside."

When I went inside, I understood Jesus in a totally different way than what I was taught. It was like they opened the door and there was such brightness.

And I said, "I'm a born-again Indian."

That's just how I felt. Now I'm a sun dancer. I pick medicines. I'm learning—something that I should have learned long ago but I didn't learn until 1992. Now I go and speak to people. Royal Bank of Canada called us twice already. These people who are managers, and they're listening, and they're touched and they're starting to understand. They're asking us, "How can we deal with reconciliation? What can we do to build that bridge?"

I said, "Start dialoguing, with anybody; with any Anishinaabe person you see, sit down with them."

First, they'll cry, because they have to release it; and then they'll start to tell you their experience. That's how it's going to be. That's the only way.

As for the priest, I told him, "If you want the Native people to go back into that church where you taught us in a bad way, if you want to build the relationship again, then go up there and tell the truth about what happened."

When I was a little girl, the church took over the reserve. We couldn't eat until they rang the bell. At six o'clock in the morning, they rang the bell—we sat down to eat. Twelve o'clock, they rang the bell and we sat, then at six o'clock. That was the start of controlling us on the reserve, and I'm telling people, until 1960, we weren't allowed to vote. Until 1960, we weren't allowed to go in a restaurant. At the beginning, when they started the reserves, they had to have permission to leave the reserve. If they left, they went to jail.[2]

They just came and yanked out the kids. My mom told me, before residential school, there was an Indian agent, a doctor, and a policeman going from house to house. Any child who was sick, they took out, and they never came back, never heard of that baby again.

When the kids went to residential school, when their parents died, they were not told. When the child died at the residential school, the parents were not told. How much damage can anybody put on a people? And now we're telling our stories; and it's like a fresh wound when we talk. Right now, I'm just shaking inside, because I'm releasing, but it's also healing.

Thank you for listening.

PART III
ASSINIBOIA AND THE ARCHIVE

Figure 40. Aerial photo of St. James Bridge with Assiniboia Indian Residential School to the east.

Survivor memories are the heart of our project. But we also decided to look at the archival records for the school. The purpose of this exploration is not to substantiate or confirm Survivor remembrances. Their expertise as knowers of their lives and their school requires no such corroboration or authentication.

What has been drawn from the archive is not objective or neutral. Andrew Woolford, a university-trained settler scholar, who has studied the violence of settler-colonial institutions, reviewed the data and made choices to link together the information he found significant. Such assessments of significance are not innocent. Choices were made based on assumptions about what the audience, and most importantly Assiniboia's Survivors, would want to hear. But these choices were also influenced by training in sociology that directs attention to certain practices in the social reproduction of institutions. Then, beyond these conscious choices, there exist those motivating factors beneath the surface that inform decisions about what information to treat as important and what to leave outside of the frame. Factors of race, gender, class, life experiences, the attraction of the familiar or the fresh—all these potentially come into play. In short, do not give this next section any more authority because of its form. It represents another engagement with memory, nothing more.

THE ARCHIVE REMEMBERS:
READING AN INSTITUTION'S MEMORY

Andrew Woolford

Institutions remember through their relationships with their human overseers and inhabitants. These memories are stored in filing cabinets, boxes, and photograph albums. They come out in diaries, newspaper stories, and letters sent to the government, church authorities, and suppliers. Assaults upon this memory also occur through these interactions. Records are destroyed, tossed in the trash, or even recycled. Theodore Fontaine tells of returning to Assiniboia in the 1970s and finding the original photo of the 1958–59 class on a pile to be thrown out. Around the same time, a woman named Muriel Macleod, who worked at the Indian and Northern Affairs Canada counselling office, discovered many squares of needlepoint created by girls at the school. These, too, were rescued. But what else was lost? The Truth and Reconciliation Commission of Canada had to struggle and strain to gain access to parts of the archival record that remained hidden in church and government buildings, behind gatekeepers reluctant to release this information. Their fight continues. With fewer resources, I explored only a portion of the Assiniboia archive—that which was publicly available.

But an institution's memory, as presented in its formal archive, should not be taken as the full history. The dates recorded below are not the only timeline of Assiniboia Residential School. The story stretches back before contact with Europeans. It rests with the grandmothers and grandfathers and is not my story to tell. What you see below is one reading of the memory of Assiniboia as an institution. I chose the documents I found to be most relevant and plotted them along a timeline. These memories have been supplemented and enhanced by what I have learned from the school's Survivors. But it is nonetheless simply one reading of this institution's memory.

Assiniboia Remembering Assiniboia

The Assiniboia Residential School opened on 2 September 1958 under the auspices of the Oblates of Mary Immaculate.[1] The Oblates operated the school until 1969, when the federal government took it over and ran it until it closed on 30 June 1973.[2] Assiniboia was the first high school for Indigenous pupils in Manitoba, though similar schools existed in other provinces, such as Saskatchewan and Ontario. Prior to its opening, Indigenous students were often sent out of province because of the lack of facilities for upper-level students in Manitoba.[3] The Roman Catholic Church in Manitoba, including Indigenous Catholics, lobbied Manitoba's Royal Commission on Education for the creation of such a school.[4] There had been prior discussion about establishing a residential high school on the Fort Alexander reservation, now the Sagkeeng First Nation.[5] The existing residential school at Fort Alexander, however, was deemed to be too outdated, and expanding it to hold high school students was impractical.[6] Instead, the former Veterans' Home on Academy Road was acquired for purposes of housing such a school. Initial suggestions for naming the new school included "Manitou Residential High School" and "Taché Residential High School."[7] An Indigenous name was felt to have "wider significance,"[8] and church authorities eventually settled on "Assiniboia Residential School."[9] It was suggested this name possessed a "great historical connotation, having designated the 116,000 sq. mile district created in 1811 by Lord Selkirk."[10] There was also agreement that the word "Indian" should not be used in the school's name "in the interests of integration."[11]

Beginning in 1915, the site and buildings of the Assiniboia School served as the Children's Home, a child care facility for children perceived to be orphaned and abandoned.[12] Plans emerged to build the Children's Home at the Academy Road address when the previous Children's Home on River Avenue was found to lack sufficient space for accommodation.[13] The two-storey, four classroom Julia Clarke School was added to the site in 1920—this is the building the Survivors refer to as the classrooms building. It also included a recreation room for the residents of the Children's Home.[14] By 1923, The Children's Home housed 339 children, a total that would rise to 400 in 1940.[15] The Children's Home was sold to transform it into a Veterans' Hospital in 1945, near the close of Second World War.[16] The Children's Home moved to two new facilities, one at 422 Assiniboine Avenue for children aged eight days to sixteen years old and the other an infants' home (for those two to ten days old) at 123 Matheson. At this time, greater emphasis was also placed on fostering the children out to families.[17]

The site came available to be used as a residential school as the postwar needs of veterans lessened. The Oblates moved into the former Veterans' Hospital in June 1958 to prepare the school for its September opening.[18] The plumbing was altered so "the two sexes may be accommodated," and the old laundry room was converted into a playroom.[19] These renovations would not be enough to make the building ready to serve as living and classroom space for Indigenous children. Moreover, by 1965, wear and tear on the building began to show. The Truth and Reconciliation Commission of Canada reports,

> A 1965 inspection described the boys' dressing room, located in the school basement, as "totally inadequate, grossly over-crowded, depressing and damp." The boys' toilet room had too few urinals, and the shower room was poorly ventilated and provided students with no privacy. The inspector described the playroom, the manual training room, the home economics kitchen, and the home economics classroom as being, respectively, "inadequate," "unsatisfactory," "extremely inadequate," and "entirely inadequate." Each was crowded and poorly ventilated. Equally critical remarks were made about the girls' playroom, and the dormitories, which were seen to be overcrowded.[20]

Reverend Omer Robidoux, OMI, who was previously principal at the Qu'Appelle Residential School in Lebret, Saskatchewan, was selected to be the first principal at Assiniboia.[21] The Grey Nuns of the Cross of Montreal joined forces with the Oblates to staff the school.[22] Together, they managed the dormitories, as well as the two grade-eight, one grade-nine, and one grade-ten classes that would occupy the four classrooms in September 1958.[23] In 1959, a grade-eleven class was added, and a grade-twelve class in 1960,[24] while grade eight was discontinued in 1962 and grade nine in 1965.[25] It was initially assumed that Assiniboia would also serve as a hostel for students taking classes at other Winnipeg schools, such as the Manitoba Institute of Technology.[26] However, in the early years of Assiniboia most students both boarded and were taught on site. By the 1960–61 school year, 130 students were enrolled at Assiniboia.[27] Assiniboia graduated its first students in 1961: Oliver Nelson (age eighteen) of Roseau River and Joe Guy Wood (age nineteen) of St. Theresa Point. At the graduation, the link between Christianity and Canadian citizenship was firmly reinforced. An Oblate newsletter, the *Indian Record*, reports: "The Most Rev. Paul Dumouchel, O.M.I., Vicar Apostolic of Keewatin, who has sent a large group of students from his Vicarage to Assiniboia school, was guest speaker; distinguishing between formal or academic instruction, he described complete education which makes good Christians good citizens and without which instruction alone would be practically worthless."[28]

Figure 41. Assiniboia Indian Residential School's first graduates, Oliver Nelson and Joe Guy Wood.

Students were predominantly Catholic, though procedures were specified for the admission of Protestant students looking to hostel at Assiniboia while attending school in Winnipeg (it is not clear that any Protestant students took up this option).[29] It is important to remember that the provisions of the 1920 amendments to the Indian Act specified that children located in communities designated to particular Christian denominations were to be sent to schools operated by those denominations.[30] Many students came to Assiniboia from Catholic day schools and residential schools. Several of these schools, such as the Fort Alexander Indian Residential School, had reputations as violent places, where too often predatory staff lurked and exploited their charges.[31] Some students were directed towards Assiniboia because they were considered strong students with good potential to succeed with advanced schooling. Others were sent out of concern that they might find themselves in trouble if they were to remain in their home communities.[32]

Figure 42. Theodore Fontaine's classroom in Fort Alexander Indian Residential School, Manitoba, Canada, c. 1949. Theodore is in the second row, visible between the two boys in the front row.

Former students describe their arrival at Assiniboia as a time of overwhelming change in their lives. Whether they had previously visited Winnipeg or not, the city presented a dramatic change from their home environs. The cars, the buildings, and the noises are all recalled as sources of uncertainty and surprise.[33] Even in the later years of the school, students experienced some disorientation when thrust into the city. In a newspaper article that dramatizes this transition, the reporter wrote of one student crossing Academy Road, "It was the first time he'd seen a car: Eddy is an Indian boy." The reporter then quotes the children's impressions of arriving in Winnipeg: "We felt like strangers from Mars when we first came here. For some of us it was the first time in a big city. With lights all over it's really groovy"; "When I got out of the plane I was just wondering about the lights and cars. I've never seen them before in my life"; "I feel there is no fresh air, to me it's stuffy that you can hardly breathe"; "most people are fat, flabby and sallow. No life, no muscle, just no health."[34]

Once the school semester had begun, students both adapted to and resisted the educational program. Whereas some found a refreshing change from the stricter and more violent residential schools from whence they transferred, others bristled against the continuation of tight regulation over their lives. In an article reprinted in this volume, Jane Glennon writes,

> Upon my arrival in the Fall of 1958 at the Assiniboia Indian Residential High School in Winnipeg, it wouldn't be long before I once again found myself disappointed with the way things were run. . . . Speaking of potential, after my first two schools, I thought this experience might prove more modern and uplifting. But the same basic rules and regulations were in place at Assiniboia. There was one difference: the order to which the sisters belonged, namely, the Grey Nuns. Along with the Oblate Fathers, they administered the school, in co-operation with the federal government. There was even an Aboriginal nun. Some students related to her but, beyond being understanding and helpful in some areas, she couldn't really obtain any concessions for us.[35]

One male student was sent home from the school when it was learned he purchased alcohol and was intoxicated while visiting a relative.[36] Others continued to experience the common residential school maladies of homesickness and loneliness and attempted to run away from Assiniboia.[37]

In these early years, before September 1967, when Assiniboia would become a hostel for Indigenous students being integrated into Winnipeg public schools, daily life was filled with course work, time in the schoolyard, occasional field trips, as well as visits to Eaton's, and nights in the dormitories. For the most part, students did not leave the school grounds. On occasion, they ventured into the River Heights neighbourhood to visit the corner store, shovel snow from driveways, or provide domestic labour in nearby houses.[38] In the 1958–59 school year, field trips were made to see the Ice Capades and the Shrine Circus, as well as a visit by the grade eight and nine classes to the Coca Cola plant on 8 June 1959, while the grade ten group was brought to a soap factory on 11 June.[39]

Classes at Assiniboia had Catholic teaching at their core. As stated in the Catholic presentation to Manitoba's Royal Commission, the belief was that "it is necessary not only that religious instruction be given to the young at certain fixed times, but also that every other subject treated be permeated with Christian thought."[40] The grade nine students at Assiniboia reiterated this belief in their newsletter:[41] "Reverend Father Alarie teaches us the most important subject, Religion. We appreciate the kindness and untiring zeal he displays in trying to show us how to live a true Christian life. He is also our literature teacher."[42] Father Robidoux played a role in the classroom as well, teaching "The Story of Indians" to the grade nines and "The Indian Act" to grade tens, both on Fridays. In 1964, the grade eleven class participated in a composition contest organized by the Knights of Columbus in which they wrote on topics such as "Come and Follow Me" and "The Greatest Among You Must Be the Servant to Others." The class also read Shakespeare's *Macbeth* and George Bernard Shaw's *Arms and the Man*.[43]

Sports were ever prominent at Assiniboia, especially among the boys. The girls would eventually embrace activities such as "jam can" curling,[44] and later baseball, basketball, and curling.[45] In the first year, the Girls' Sports reporter noted, "we have to admit that sports hasn't been too popular among the girls this year. Maybe it because *[sic]* everything is so new in the Assiniboia School. We promise that next year it will be different, and that we will have interesting sports to report."[46] For the boys, funding for a hockey rink was allocated on 5 November 1958,[47] and the boys' hockey team would be a force in local hockey leagues for years to come. However, the lack of a gymnasium was keenly felt and the students largely focused on outdoor activities.[48] In addition to hockey, the boys excelled at cross-country and football.[49] In 1962, for example, the Assiniboia hockey team won the Junior B championship of Manitoba for the third consecutive year.[50] It was not until 1966 that a chapel and gymnasium were officially opened at the school.[51]

A chapel and gym will be erected this spring at ASSINIBOINE HIGH SCHOOL for Indians, in Winnipeg City, at the cost of $166,000, paid by the federal government. The new building will be located south of the classroom block.

Figure 43. Drawing of Assiniboia chapel and gym, c. 1965.

From 9:00 p.m. onward, the students would be in bed in their dormitories. In the early years, the dormitories had approximately fifteen beds per room, though a divider rather than a wall may have separated rooms.[52] It is at this time that they would have one of their more negative experiences within the River Heights community. As they lay in the dark, people in passing cars would harass the students from their sleep, hollering mocking "war whoops" towards the dormitories, as noted in Theodore Fontaine's chapter.[53] A night watchman was hired for the school in 1960,[54] perhaps to help prevent these unwanted night visits, but former students also attest that the police might have been asked to give greater attention to this matter.[55]

Like many Indigenous boarding schools across North America, Assiniboia at least paid lip service to establishing a "family atmosphere."[56] One of the means for fostering this atmosphere was holiday events based on key days in the Christian calendar. The December school newsletter, for example, was typically graced with cover art depicting the nativity scene.[57] While many students returned home for the holidays, some were not able to make the journey.

This "family atmosphere" also included preparation for an assimilated family life complete with prescribed gender roles. The female students at Assiniboia took part in Home Economics classes, where they engaged in activities such as embroidering, knitting, sewing, baking, and preparing a fancy dinner to celebrate the principal's birthday, complete with white tablecloth, silverware, and candles.[58] The male students, in contrast, were engaged in typical masculine activities, including sports such as football and cadet corps, which involved drilling and weapons training. On occasions like the Winter Carnival, the cadets would display their skills. Reporter Theda Bradshaw, who appears to have covered events at Assiniboia somewhat regularly, describes the following at the 1962 carnival: "The school corps of 20 uniformed members marched down the ice in varying formations. Affiliated with the 39th Regiment, the boys have weekly practice drill and a lecture at Fort Osborne."[59]

Discipline at the school came in the form of military and religious instruction, as well as further habituating students to dominant gender norms. Through such activity, the Oblates sought to shape student souls to reflect both Canadian citizenry and Catholic standards.[60] Principal Robidoux's vision of the perfected student is captured in his editorial advice on preparing for Easter exams, which was printed in the school's newsletter: "This motivation must be similar to the motivation which prompted Christ to die for us—LOVE. Our love must be outgoing and unselfish. It must inspire us to perfect ourselves as individuals and thus help perfect the society in which we live."[61]

While these forms of discipline sought to positively effect change upon the student, more negative strategies of disciplinary punishment were also in evidence, though perhaps not to the extent they were in the schools from which the students had transferred.

Assiniboia Cadets Receive Annual Spring Inspection

Winnipeg's Assiniboia High School Cadet Corps had its annual inspection this spring, culminating the entire years training in basic drill, rifle handling, national survival and map using.

Demonstrations of these newly acquired skills and of gymnastics were given during this, the 6th annual inspection of the group.

Inspecting the man on parade were Lt. Colonel W. Barrit and his aide de campe, accompanied by Lt. C. R. Palmer of the Cadet Training Staff.

Figure 44. Assiniboia cadets receive inspection, c. 1965.

Assiniboia appears to have provided satisfactorily nutritious food in its refectory. A 1962 report from the regional dietician notes, "The food is fairly attractive in color, texture and variety. The nutritional value of the menus seem adequate except perhaps in eggs. Eggs are not well accepted by the students now and they are getting them about once a week. Mr. LeDoyen has trouble getting them to accept vegetables also. He serves them raw and in stews and soups, and there are 1–2 servings daily on the menu. The students receive a lot of fresh fruit, usually 1–2 times daily."[62] However, this quality of food should not be attributed to government largesse. Throughout the history of Assiniboia, food costs were a distinct concern. The federal government made little allowance for the cost differences faced by a school with older students, expecting them to run according to the same per diem costs as residential schools for younger age groups.[63] Cost overruns for food are noted in many years of the school's operation, and the federal government continually chastised Assiniboia principals for their lack of economy. For example, Father Robidoux's overexpenditures for food and clothing in 1959 were to be recovered from the 1960 budget, lest the Church would have to reimburse the government for the excess amount.[64] This problem would persist across many years. In 1968, the government accused Father Chaput, a former teacher then serving as principal, of ordering "top quality" items through a buying agency rather than seeking the best prices available. The buying agency would later intervene in this dispute, noting that the school's cook demanded certain brands and quality food items rather than seeking nutrition on the cheap.[65] Father Chaput would add, "If the Department wants these children integrated it is a much more costly operation and I am not going to stint on the quantity or quality of food and clothing."[66]

The topic of "integration" loomed large over the middle years of Assiniboia's existence. In the 1960s, it became difficult for the Canadian government to continue to deny the social inequalities experienced by Indigenous peoples. The civil rights movement in the United States influenced thinking on the question of discrimination in Canada, but often resulted in embrace of a notion of equality that threatened to erase Aboriginal and treaty rights. The so-called 1969 "White Paper" put forward by Pierre Trudeau's Liberal government to eliminate the Indian Act was the culmination of this thinking. It was widely criticized by Indigenous people for failing to consider the concerns raised by Indigenous leaders when they were consulted prior to the release of the White Paper, which was seen as an attempt to immerse Indigenous people within Canadian society so that their cultures and territorial claims would simply disappear.[67]

The push toward an undifferentiated "equality" through integration was felt early on with regard to Indigenous schooling. The 1961 special joint committee of the Senate and the House of Commons and the 1963 Glassco Commission both recommended the closing of "Indian" schools and the integration of Indigenous students into the public school system. The 1966 Hawthorne Report, which influenced the development of the White Paper, also called for the closing of schools.[68] The idea of closing residential schools and integrating Indigenous students into public schools faced expected opposition from the Roman Catholic Church, which often voiced how concerned Indigenous people were about its possible implementation.[69] For example, an *Indian Record*[70] editorial positively frames the 1920 Indian Act amendments allowing denominations to claim Indigenous children from specific communities for their own schools. As the editorial argues, "Over the years the freedom of the Churches in serving the Indian Population's educational needs has been severely curtailed. Although the Indian Act provides for denominational schools on all Indian reserves, little attention has been paid to the safeguard of the religious privileges of students transferred to public schools."[71] In October of 1962, Clive Linklater, an Indigenous political advocate who held executive, consulting, and leadership roles with the National Indian Brotherhood and the Indian Association of Alberta, claimed that integration for the "Indian" was little different than assimilation: "The meaning the Indian people derive [from integration] is that of 'assimilation,' that is: the abolition of all Indian schools, the doing away of all Indian Reserves, the extinguishing of Indian culture, and the abrogation of Treaties and Treaty rights. The Indian people, when fully 'integrated' or 'assimilated' will then have finally vanished."[72]

The push towards integration soon transformed Assiniboia. As early as 1965, Deputy Minister of Citizenship and Immigration G.W. Isbister wrote to Reverend A. Lizée, Provincial Superior of the Oblates, to complain that "Over the past seven years the original purpose of the school has not been achieved, and the tendency has been for it to become more and more a segregated school."[73] This alleged oversight was addressed in 1967 when the school was converted into a hostel for seventy-nine students. The expressed rationale for the transition to a hostel was framed in a discourse of equal rights and opportunity. The Indian Affairs Branch stated that it wanted to give the Indian students the same choice in courses available to students at public schools. But integration was also a primary matter of concern: "Branch officials say integration with non-Indian students at the high school level will break the social barriers through association with the non-Indian way of life and thus promote better understanding on both parts."[74]

The Assiniboia school administration sought to find space for their boarders at Winnipeg Catholic high schools, such as the St. Boniface Diocesan High School, which accepted twenty students, the Convent of the Sacred Heart in Charleswood, which accepted eleven, and the St. Charles Convent, which accepted seventeen. Other students were dispersed to schools such as Gordon Bell, Kelvin, and Vincent Massey.[75] The classrooms were subsequently used primarily for evening study, and no longer held daytime classes of students.[76] The school continued to supply clothing for students. The clothing list for one female student included: "1 rain coat, 1 winter coat, 1 ski jacket, 2 pairs slacks, 2 pairs hose or leotards, 1 pr winter boots, 1 pr rain boots, 1 cardigan, 1 woolen shell, 3 brassieres, 3 prs panties, 3 half slips, 4 prs knee hoses, 1 pantie girdle, 4 blouses, 3 summer skirts, 3 winter skirts, 1 pr gloves, 1 pr mitts, 2 prs shoes, 2 prs runners, 1 gym suit," while a male student received: "2 prs pants, 3 dress shirts, 5 prs stockings, 3 sweat shirts, 4 underwear shorts, 1 jacket, 1 pr shoes, 1 gym suit, 1 pr runners." Both were to be provided a parka, sweater, and overcoat prior to winter.[77]

Integration was not a smooth transition for Assiniboia's boarders. Many faced discrimination within Winnipeg public schools. Martina Therese Fisher recalls being ignored by her teachers: "The teachers never talked to me, students never talked to me. I felt singled out. I was, I was lonely, I was scared. There was nobody to help me with my work. I couldn't wait to be eighteen years old."[78] Emblematic of this discrimination was the experience of the ten Indigenous runners who were selected to carry the ceremonial torch for the 1967 Pan-Am Games in Winnipeg (see Charlie Nelson chapter, this volume). The student runners carried the torch 800 kilometres along a traditional

Indigenous message route.[79] But at the threshold of the stadium, just when they thought they would carry the torch to the officials, the torch was handed to a non-Indigenous athlete. One of the runners, Patrick Bruyere, recalls, "So, we hand them over, and we came outside, and we thought we were gonna bring in the torch, and then one of the Indian Affairs fellas says, 'Thank you very much, boys. There's breakfast waiting for you around the corner there, Pancake House.' And then they, they gave this torch to this athlete, eh, and he took it in, and that was it. So, we didn't think anything, eh. Like I said, in boarding school you did as you were told and that was it, you didn't ask questions."[80]

* * *

Assiniboia was a space of colonial ambivalence. For some students, the school afforded them an environment so different from their previous schools that their school experience was largely positive. Here, the students were able to develop critical perspectives on residential schools, Canada's treatment of Indigenous peoples, and the so-called Indian problem. For example, in a May 1962 meeting with a group of Assiniboia students, Theda Bradshaw presented them with "several controversial statements about the Indian." These included a statement by Clive Linklater that "the Indian feels he is not given sufficient consultation in matters affecting his own life and destiny." In response, students took contrasting positions, one arguing that "the Indians are not ready to be consulted" while another countered "the white man always has the last word." Likewise, when presented with the very immediate debate about Indigenous integration into white schools, the students further demonstrated varied insight into the topic, including some very critical of settler colonial domination: "When Indians go to public schools they don't seem to be accepted because white people don't want their children mixing with us. Indians drop out of public schools very quickly"; "Integration does have good points for it helps us to get along with other races. This gets the

Indian out of his own social circle and gives him a broader outlook"; "Only partial integration is needed. . . . We think there's something better than integration. The Indian population is increasing and what we need is more land"; "The main problem of the Indian is the white man. Integration is not the solution."[81]

In another example, Assiniboia students in 1967 organized and hosted a conference titled "Meet the Indian." This was the "centennial project" for Assiniboia students, celebrating 100 years since the founding of Canada. High-school students, Indigenous and non-Indigenous, were invited from across Winnipeg. Rather than simply encourage a patriotic celebration of Canadian settler colonialism, the students engaged with pressing social issues. They discussed topics related to education, residential schools, Indian Affairs, racial prejudice, alcoholism, and the question of integration.[82] The students endorsed a resolution to promote exchanges of students between Indigenous and non-Indigenous schools, promoting these exchanges as a means for overcoming racial segregation.[83]

Students also were prepared for leadership. In the 1963–64 school year a student council was formed "to give the boys more responsibility and to have to organize themselves better."[84] As well, students could take leadership roles through sports, cadets, and student associations. While these were opportunities for empowerment, they also were consistent with a shift in Oblate policy towards Indigenous education that emphasized higher education that would encourage Indigenous children to become leaders who "will save the Indian Race."[85] This message continued throughout the history of Assiniboia, such as when in 1966 Archbishop Flahiff advised the five school graduates "to forget past grievances, and to take full advantage of the opportunities they now have to their rightful place as leaders in Canadian society."[86]

Debate and discussion also occurred through classes and clubs at Assiniboia, such as through the school's MAMI (Missionary Association of Mary Immaculate) association, a voluntary organization directed towards having its participants emulate the spirit and mission of the Oblates. For example, the 1964 MAMI group reports discussion of questions such as "What are the advantages and disadvantages of having women as councillors or chiefs?" The MAMI correspondent reporting to the school's newsletter slyly noted, "The disadvantages for this question, as given by several boys, were patiently accepted by the girls."[87]

Letters cont'd

Dear Robert:
        I
        I would like to thank you and everyone at Assiniboia High for invi-
ting us all to "Meet the Indian" on April 22nd. I've never been so glad
I attended any function as I was about the conference last Saturday. It
was beneficial in every way. We all learned so much. The main thing I
learned was that there was such a place as Assiniboia High. I'm ashamed
of not knowing about it before. Your school and the students in it are a
credit to the community. "Meet the Indian" has got to be one of the best
centennial projects this year. I felt I got to know you people better and
appreciate more the Indian culture.

        The dance in the evening was really something, too. I wish the kids
at our school had the spirit you do, to get up and dance, instead of just
standing around. It was good to see everyone on the floor. We also
could do well with something artistic like that fabuluos mural at the bac
back of the stage. All we've got is dull gray curtains. The scene really looked good and the band couldn't have had a better background. And
the powwow, what better way could there be to get a dance started? Everyone liked the bright, colorful costumes, too.

        From start to finish, the conference was a most interesting experi-
ence. Once again, thank you.

                          Yours truly
                          Lynn Zayshley
                          Gordon Bell High

Hi Everyone!

        I felt that just shaking hands with all of you just wasn't enough.
A fuller more meaningful "thank you" was needed, so I decided to put it
in writing.

        But writing my thanks just doesn't seem adequate. It doesn't expres
my wonderment at how marvelous the conference was! It was just "too
much"! I've never spent a more fantastically enjoyable and educational
day! Everything was so well-planned and beautifully done that I'm sure
it not only amazed me, but each white student that attended.

        Thank you so much for giving me the chance to attend such a terrific
conference, to meet so many great kids, and to learn more about the Indian than I could ever imagine

                          Love, many thanks
                          Brenda Crushko

Figure 45. Letter to the Editor printed in *Assiniboia Highlights*, 1967.

Figure 46. Header Image from the 1958–59 Assiniboia Newsletter.

At the same time, Survivors have also described troubling episodes at the school. Notable among these was the attempted rape of Violet Rupp Cook in the school gymnasium by one of the Assiniboia supervisors. She was able to fight him off, but was nonetheless distressed by the incident: "I didn't know what to do. I was, I was afraid, I was just shaking, I went, I went back to the dorms. I didn't tell anybody I was so, I felt so ashamed. I didn't tell my supervisor, I didn't tell anyone. I didn't tell any of the girls that were there."[88]

Assiniboia closed on 30 June 1973. Economic reasons were cited as the primary motivation for shuttering this and three other residential schools in Manitoba. It was also noted that Indigenous parents wanted to have their children educated closer to home. The main building was demolished in 1984, making way for a $5-million RCMP forensics laboratory. The federal government was criticized for letting the former building fall to ruin rather than ensuring its proper upkeep.[90]

Assiniboia, Guy Residences closed

WINNIPEG — The four Indian residential schools in Manitoba are to be closed, two at the end of this school term and two by mid-1974, a spokesman of the department of Indian affairs said May 17th.

Bill Thomas, department regional director, said the Assiniboia Residential School, 621 Academy Rd., and the Guy Hill Residential School, at The Pas, are to be closed at the end of this school term.

Mr. Thomas said the Portage Residential School, in Portage la Prairie, and the McKay Residential School, in Dauphin, are to be closed next year.

A hint at the fate of residential schools in Dauphin and Portage la Prairie came May 16 in the House of Commons. Indian Affairs Minister Jean Chretien, in answer to a question, said the schools might be closed.

Mr. Thomas gave economic reasons, a lack of enrolment, and the wish of the Indian people to have their children closer to home as the main reasons behind the decision to close the schools.

The two schools being closed this year were operating at "half capacity or less," he said.   •

Figure 47. Article on the closing of the Assiniboia Residence, 1973.

Assiniboia is an important school in the history of the Indian residential school system because it forces us to wrestle with the complexity of this system. Engaging Assiniboia requires that we understand the variety of residential school experiences, while not using those that are on the surface positive, or at least not as outwardly violent as what has been captured in Truth and Reconciliation Commission of Canada (TRC) testimony and elsewhere, to somehow absolve the system. Assiniboia was a respite from earlier violence for many students. It was also a place where new friendships and familial relationships were formed with fellow students. But it was nonetheless part of a system designed and enacted to destroy Indigenous identities, eliminate Indigenous nations, and ensure the unquestioned dispossession of Indigenous territories.

The TRC has referred to Canada's residential school system as "cultural genocide"; many Survivors, scholars, and others simply use the unqualified term, genocide.[91] The fact that students at Assiniboia enjoyed playing hockey, grew critical of the Indian residential school system and settler society, or experienced principals and teachers who provided them support does not mean that the genocidal process stopped at the boundaries of the Assiniboia campus. Assiniboia was founded upon a notion of the Indian problem, whereby the intended goal of the school was to fashion a future group of leaders who would return to their communities and help integrate Indians into the fabric of settler Canadian society.[92] That many of the students did not become emissaries of assimilation and integration is testament to their resilience. While several found career success, they, as well as others, became different leaders than what was initially hoped for by the Catholic leaders who dreamed up Assiniboia. Many have returned to their Indigenous languages and teachings and have become a vanguard of Indigenous resurgence in Winnipeg, Manitoba, and beyond.

PART IV
STAFF REMEMBRANCES

MEET THE STAFF

1. Reverend Father O. Robidoux, OMI ....Principal

2. Reverend Father L. Alarie, OMI ....Senior Teacher

3. Reverend Father M. Rio, OMI ....Missionary

4. Reverend Sister B. Forest ....Superior

5. Reverend Sister M. Constantin ....Girls' Matron

6. Reverend Sister C. Tougas ....Teacher

7. Reverend Sister A. Pepin ....Teacher

8. Reverend Sister E. Ell ....Cook

9. Reverend Sister A. Decoine ....Nurse

10. Mr. J. Lambert ....Teacher

11. Mrs. B. Lavresult ....Home Ec. Instructor

12. Mr. G. Heshka ....Manual Training Instructor

13. Miss Lorraine Ballagarde ....Music Teacher

14. Mr. Luc Marchildon ....Boys' Supervisor

15. Miss B. Acoose ....General

16. Mr. Laurent Marchildon ....Assistant Boys' Supervisor

17. Mr. J.R. Glenn ....Engineer

18. Mr. L. Champagne ....Engineer

19. Mr. G.W. Fraser ....Engineer

20. Mr. S. Filmore ....Engineer

21. Mr. A. Lamothe ....Night Watchman

22. Miss E. Lerat ....Seamstress

23. Mrs. A. Nanowin ....Assistant Cook

24. Miss Jane Kakeychewan ....Kitchen Helper

25. Miss M. Desjarlais ....Kitchen Helper

26. Mr. L. Legal ....Maintenance

27. Mr. A. Fillion ....Maintenance

Figure 48. Staff list from 1958–59 Assiniboia Newsletter.

The decision to include staff voices in this volume was made by the Survivor Governing Council for the project, a group of Assiniboia Survivors who guided the initial activities that resulted in a 2017 reunion, this volume, and the continued efforts to create a commemorative marker and gathering place on the former Assiniboia grounds, now under the auspices of the Assiniboia Indian Residential School Legacy Group.

Staff voices were welcomed because the Survivor Governing Council understood there to be multiple perspectives on Assiniboia. Not only did they see students from different eras as having different perspectives, they felt staff and neighbours did, as well. Some have maintained relations with teachers since they departed from Assiniboia, and invited them to attend the 2017 reunion, where many of the chapters that comprise this volume were initially recorded.

I LOVED THE STUDENTS
LIKE THEY WERE MY KID BROTHERS AND SISTERS

Sister Jean Ell
Worked at Assiniboia, 1958–60

I was part of the original group of staff hired in advance of the opening of the Assiniboia Indian Residential School. My first job was to set up the kitchen and prepare to feed about 100 teenagers and all the staff of the school. I was twenty-one years old and had just made my vows to the Grey Nuns when I was assigned to Assiniboia.

Before coming to Assiniboia, I had worked not quite a year in Fort Frances in a residential school there, and then I got very sick. The doctors didn't want me to stay there because I was allergic to the sulphur in the air from the paper mill.

Assiniboia was much more open than the Fort Frances school. That school went only to grade eight. At Assiniboia, they were all teenagers and in high school.

For me, as the head cook, the biggest difference was the freedom I enjoyed in the kitchen. In Fort Frances, the priest who was directing the school looked after the purchasing of food within a strict budget. The local RCMP officers supplemented our choice and variety of foods by supplying venison. At Assiniboia, I was in charge of the kitchen. I ordered the food, I bought what I wanted, and made the menus.

Ted Fontaine often talks about his childhood experiences during ten years at the Fort Alexander Indian Residential School. He describes how badly the students were treated and how poorly they were fed. When I came to Assiniboia, I didn't know about their past experiences, but I could see that these kids enjoyed the meals I made for them.

I didn't have any formal training in cooking, but my mom was an excellent cook. She was often sick and so she taught me how to cook even when I was just four or five years old. I followed her instructions and cooked just as she taught me. We lived on a farm, so we had milk, eggs, cheese, whipping cream, and all those goodies, and a big garden.

Figure 49. Sister Jean Ell at Assiniboia Indian Residential School, c. 1958.

We had everything at hand, so we always had solid meals. The men were working hard outdoors in the fields and we had to feed them well, so they had the energy to do the work. That was my upbringing as a cook, and that's how I fed the students.

At Assiniboia, we always had meat, potatoes, vegetables, dessert— always dessert—and salads. Especially at noon, I would make soup and salads and different things that wouldn't be too heavy, that wouldn't bog them down so that they couldn't learn or study in the afternoon. I didn't want to put them to sleep. You had to balance the meal so they would be able to study. And when they would go outside to play hockey or baseball or to run around, they needed plenty of energy.

I had two very good helpers. The older one was Bernice (I don't remember her family name), and the second one was Dorothy Cook. I remember them so well. That's fifty-nine years ago! Fifty-nine years seems like a long time, and yet, it seems like yesterday.

Figure 50. Sister Ell and Father Alarie at the 2017 Assiniboia Reunion.

I often packed up students' lunches as a picnic. They would take it to Assiniboine Park, and they'd have lunch over there. They'd have a bit of a break, and then an hour or two later they'd all come back and go to classes. We did all kinds of things that would give them a break, help them get to know the city, and just know how people live. They'd see that there's a bigger world. They were also allowed to go out and shovel snow and earn some cash. The priest we had, Father Robidoux, was really good about that.

Father Robidoux was the principal and the director of the place. He was very open and understood that Aboriginal children had not been well treated, and so he made sure the school was run in a way that was very open. He was adamant that they were to be treated well. The teachers they had were really good and very caring.

To be surrounded by so many young people was a real delight. It was a very good experience for me as a young nun. What I appreciated the most was the youthfulness of these young people and their eagerness to learn. Whatever they did—if it was sports or it was studying—they really were into it. During my time there they had all kinds of sports. They had one young man who won relay and other races. You could see him practising in the yard. He was tall and would always win. They loved hockey and baseball and all those sports, but they especially loved food.

I also enjoyed the fact that they loved everything that I made and ate everything up. I never had leftovers. That was impossible; they would come back for seconds.

I loved the students like they were my kid brothers and sisters. I am thinking especially about the boys because the girls were so quiet and calm, whereas the boys were all over the place. They kept me laughing, and because I have brothers, it's easier for me to understand them.

Figure 51. Photographs of teachers from David Montana Wesley's scrapbook.

At Assiniboia, there appeared to be more freedom for the students. I know they were careful to separate the boys and girls, but the students did see each other and had more of a social life. They make fun of that, but Father Robidoux made sure they behaved themselves.

We did our best to watch over them, in a way, because they were without their parents. We wanted to protect them and make sure they were safe. We all lived there, so we tried to create a comfortable home for the students. I remember Sister Tougas, Cecile Tougas, taught at Assiniboia. She was an excellent teacher, and she was so dedicated. If some of the students were behind when they arrived, she would give them extra classes after school, and help them out until they were caught up with everybody else—she was very, very dedicated.

I still know Father Alarie, who taught for ten years in this school, and he was also very dedicated. He's a very soft-spoken person, not pushy. Everybody would listen because he's so gentle. He was the type who said what he had to say. He loved teaching at Assiniboia; I think all the staff did. Even today, sixty years later, both Father Alarie and I remember many of the Assiniboia students by name. We share little stories of their experiences, and some of the students are still in touch with us after all these years.

I was sorry to be reassigned by the Grey Nuns after only two years at Assiniboia. One of the sisters in the kitchen in Gravelbourg, Saskatchewan, got sick, so I was sent there and helped them out until she was back. And then they sent me to the kitchen in St. Boniface Hospital, and by that time it was time for me to go to Montreal for my final vows. The Grey Nuns sent me to school as well. I got my master's in social work, and worked for thirty-five years with the mentally ill. I continued to work with young teenagers and young adults all my life as a result of my experience of having worked with young people before.

But I never stopped cooking. I love making cakes and desserts. When Ted Fontaine comes to visit, it is my little joy to feed him again and send him home with a box of baked desserts.

Father Alarie and I both attended the Assiniboia reunion. It was a delight to visit the old grounds and to be reunited with so many students we remember so well. There were media covering the reunion, and I was interviewed by CBC. They asked me where I was when I learned that the residential schools were in trouble, that stories of abuse and neglect were coming out, and they asked how I felt on hearing about this.

I first heard about it when I was travelling to Saskatoon. I was on an airplane, and a gentleman was beside me, and he said, "You're a nun?" And I said, "Yes," because I was dressed in full regalia. He said something about these residential schools being in the news. And I said, "What are you talking about?" I had not heard. I was working, so I didn't always hear the news that was going on. He said that they're saying that the residential schools were bad experiences for the students.

I don't remember the whole conversation. But I thought, "Oh my goodness, I've been to two residential schools. Did I do something wrong?" You immediately start questioning yourself. I was kind of shocked, because I had no idea that some schools were not properly run. Kids can't learn if they don't have food in their stomach. If they're attending to a growling stomach, their brains can't function.

In later years, I heard much more about the terrible experiences students had endured in other Indian residential schools, especially when they were younger, just small children. It's just incomprehensible that a government would try to destroy a nation. Why? I've often asked myself that.

When I arrived at the reunion, I went into the classrooms building where a woman introduced herself as having been there when I was there. She said, "I went to university," and her daughter was beside her, and she said, "So did I," and there was a little kid running around alongside them. You see, that's three generations now that have gone through school.

These are the young people we were looking after in those days. I think when you treat the youth right, they come out right. They live their lives to the fullest, and have a really good life regardless of what they do. It is shocking to realize that so many students who attended Indian residential schools never had that chance.

So many of the Assiniboia students I remember went on to achieve tremendous success in their professional and personal lives. Ted Fontaine, Joe Guy Wood, Oliver Nelson, Phil Fontaine, Lloyd McKay, Jane McCallum, Pauline Wood, and so many more, they went on to make a difference in the lives of their communities and people across Canada. We were always so proud of all the students at Assiniboia.

Dedication

TO

OUR

FORMER

PRINCIPAL

A GREAT OLE MAN

A great big load he has to bear
but what it weighs he does not care,
He'll keep on going through water and bush
And sometimes giving his load a push.
Branches tear his clothes apart
But always fail to reach his heart.
He'll take his load where he has to
Although through hardships he must go.
He'll get it through no matter what
Friend, what a great ole man is that.
Who guides you through the hardest times
Though he has none of nickels and dimes.

When hope is lost and not in view
This great ole man just talks to you.
And what he says brings you new light
For he keeps saying "future's bright".
Now and then he laughs and plays
And recalls us when he prays,
A great ole man, we'll all agree
Was sent to earth for you and me,
His work in here may worthy be to
Call it "honor" for all or you
But take time off for him to pray
Yet he gets time, his nights and days,
Bow your weary heads in silence
And show that we are all his Friends.
A great ole man, and all he wants
Is only we to understand.

Matt Mason

3

Figure 52. Dedication to Father Robidoux in 1967 Keewatin Yearbook.

WE WON MORE THAN WE LOST

Luc Marchildon
Worked at Assiniboia, 1958–65

Transcribed from an oral interview.

I was the boys' supervisor. I spent seven years at Assiniboia, and I enjoyed it very much—working in sports with these boys.

It started with the fall training. It was training for hockey. I managed the hockey school here for seven years. The first year, I had to build the playing field. The previous field was full of bumps and all kinds of obstacles. We levelled it off to make a football field.

I started working on that in the summer before the school opened. There were two of us on the staff: the principal, Father Robidoux, and myself. We worked with pick and shovel hard all summer.

Then in the fall when the snow started coming, we built hockey rinks across the football field; these rinks were outdoor rinks, of course. There was one big rink for the boys to play intramural sports within the city, and then there was a second rink for practices. And then we had a third hockey rink for the girls.

All that was built in the snow in October of the first year. Then in the spring, I had to take that down so we could play baseball. I was involved in all that in 1958 and 1959; and then by the time I'd put the teams together, I had three teams here competing in the Winnipeg Hockey Association.

The team that I coached was a junior team with nineteen- and twenty-year-old young men, and I had to also take on boys who were sixteen because we didn't have enough players. But we did win, in 1960, the Manitoba championship in Junior B hockey.

Then we won five years in a row, and I coached all five teams. I'm very proud of having done that, and very proud of these players.

We also played football. I coached a team. We had a school team, because we didn't have enough players to do anything else. We played

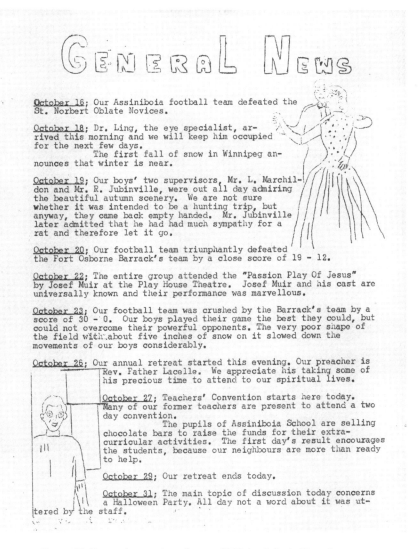

GENERAL NEWS

October 16; Our Assiniboia football team defeated the St. Norbert Oblate Novices.

October 18; Dr. Ling, the eye specialist, arrived this morning and we will keep him occupied for the next few days.
     The first fall of snow in Winnipeg announces that winter is near.

October 19; Our boys' two supervisors, Mr. L. Marchildon and Mr. R. Jubinville, were out all day admiring the beautiful autumn scenery. We are not sure whether it was intended to be a hunting trip, but anyway, they came back empty handed. Mr. Jubinville later admitted that he had had much sympathy for a rat and therefore let it go.

October 20; Our football team triumphantly defeated the Fort Osborne Barrack's team by a close score of 19 - 12.

October 22; The entire group attended the "Passion Play Of Jesus" by Josef Muir at the Play House Theatre. Josef Muir and his cast are universally known and their performance was marvellous.

October 23; Our football team was crushed by the Barrack's team by a score of 30 - 0. Our boys played their game the best they could, but could not overcome their powerful opponents. The very poor shape of the field with about five inches of snow on it slowed down the movements of our boys considerably.

October 26; Our annual retreat started this evening. Our preacher is Rev. Father Lacelle. We appreciate his taking some of his precious time to attend to our spiritual lives.

October 27; Teachers' Convention starts here today. Many of our former teachers are present to attend a two day convention.
     The pupils of Assiniboia School are selling chocolate bars to raise the funds for their extra-curricular activities. The first day's result encourages the students, because our neighbours are more than ready to help.

October 29; Our retreat ends today.

October 31; The main topic of discussion today concerns a Halloween Party. All day not a word about it was uttered by the staff.

Figure 53. General news item from a 1960 Assiniboia Newsletter.

in a league against Stonewall and all those towns surrounding Stonewall. We played against out-of-town teams, because we weren't strong enough to play in the city. The Winnipeg teams were much stronger.

Figure 54. Members of the Assiniboia hockey team, seen outside in winter, 1959.

Figure 55. Members of the Assiniboia hockey team celebrate their victory in the Manitoba Junior B Championship, 1960.

We won the football championship against Stonewall. I still remember that day.

Then we had a lot of track and field. These Aboriginal boys were very good in running, so I had them running in all kinds of track events, and they were very good.

We also had baseball, though it was played off-season and we never played in any championships.

But we also had a gym built the last two years I was here. Then we started basketball and gymnastics.

I enjoyed those years very much.

The girls were on one side, and I handled all the boys on the other side. And, of course, I had an assistant with me to run the boys' side.

Those were very enjoyable years, and I have since met quite a few of my older students who were here in the fifties and sixties—I met them at the reunion. There's a few I haven't seen for fifty-five years.

For example, there's Ted Fontaine. He was with me; he was one of my super hockey players in 1958 and 1959, but then he decided to finish his high school in Pine Falls. So, I missed him. He would have been my top hockey player.

You know, one year we had eighty boys, and out of those eighty boys we had three teams. To choose fifteen players out of eighty boys, we had to really work hard. And they came out. I made them train very hard. That's the only thing that the boys were telling me after fifty-five years. I had them training very hard, and they accepted it and worked, and they won.

I can't remember all the towns we played in. We challenged certain towns for the Manitoba championship, and in those years we had to challenge before we would get challenged. We won more than we lost, because five years in a row we were Manitoba champs in the Junior B groups. But we also challenged sometimes some of the Junior A teams in the city. And we matched them quite well.

I had some players who should have played professionally, but because they had to concentrate on schoolwork, the administration decided it was better that they do their schoolwork and put aside the hockey.

I did have some very fine hockey players here who could have played professional hockey. But football, not so much, nor baseball. They were too light. These boys were not very big and they were slim. They were sixteen, seventeen years old, and not heavy enough to play football against the city teams.

They also did other things that I enjoyed, like a little bit of drama, and on Saturdays and Sundays, dancing. Saturday nights I would supervise that with some of the teachers, you know, supervising some of the activities. It was very good.

One of the things I enjoyed very much was Father Robidoux's system. He had done this at other schools before, in Lebret, Saskatchewan, where he had started a high school. Every second Sunday, twice a month, we'd gather all the students in the cafeteria—that was the hall in those days—we had no gymnasium, no hall. We'd gather there, and there were discussions, round tables, the boys and the girls together.

They would discuss problems on the Indian reserves, and I enjoyed listening to all those discussions.

You know, when I left here, I didn't come back very much. The school closed in 1973, and I wasn't here. I was teaching at Collège de Saint-Boniface.

Of course, I was so busy that I didn't have time to come visit. And some of these students were too young. They couldn't remember me, they didn't know me, so I never did come back very much after 1965.

Figure 56. Father Robidoux, Le Bret Indian Residential School, May 1951.

PART V
NEIGHBOURS

Figure 57. Cornerstone from the original building, 2019.

The Assiniboia Indian Residential School was located at 621 Academy Road, which is part of Winnipeg's affluent River Heights neighbourhood. The school's playing field backed onto Wellington Crescent, one of the wealthiest areas of the city. This was an unusual place for a residential school, and we know of no other such school being situated in a neighbourhood where differences in socio-economic status were quite so stark.

Assiniboia students were noticed in the neighbourhood, often as snow shovellers or domestic workers. However, the school was quite often unknown to other residents. To this day, many people in Winnipeg are unaware that a residential school was located within the city limits. This is why the Survivors ask, "Did you see us?" This volume is part of their effort to make this fact known.

The voices presented here are just a few from those who knew, or knew little, of the Indian residential school in Winnipeg.

I WAS UNAWARE

Gary Robson

Reunion Volunteer and Winnipeg Resident

Transcribed from an oral interview.

My personal experience with the Assiniboia Indian Residential School is very limited. As a matter of fact, I only became aware that an Indian residential school existed in Winnipeg within the last couple of years through some (now) friends who are Survivors—former students of the school. For most of my life I was completely oblivious, not only to Assiniboia Indian Residential School, but to the residential school system in general, except for the fact that I had an uncle who was the principal of Cecilia Jeffrey Indian Residential School just outside of Kenora, Ontario. And, I used to spend summer holiday time there. As a real youngster—I was five or six years old at the time—I was completely unaware of the reality of what was going on and didn't understand what was happening or why it was happening.

I learned about residential schools in general fairly recently. The history of Aboriginal people in Canada, I also learned about as an adult. It never came up in any of my public school or university education.

I got married in 1970. By about 1975, my wife and I decided it was time to start a family, and it wasn't happening. We began to look into the idea of adoption. At the time, the thing that was in the news and the thing that you did hear about was Vietnamese boat people who needed support, and about what was happening with new families trying to escape the aftermath of war in their country. We began to inquire into that, but soon after my wife became pregnant. We had two kids, but we never lost sight of the idea that adoption might be a good thing to do. In the very late 1970s, we contacted an adoption agency in Manitoba and talked about it. They said that the greatest need for adoptions in Manitoba was among Aboriginal children. Being unaware of the historical background, we thought, "Well, if that's the need." We had never heard of the "sixties scoop" and no mention of it was ever made. We adopted an infant who is now a mature woman, a member of the Berens River First Nation (Mememwi-ziibiing), and we began through our daughter to become involved, because we wanted her to be aware of her culture and her background.

We began to do things like attending powwows, and taking her to Sagkeeng First Nation for sweats. As a result of that, we became aware of Aboriginal culture in a way we had never been before. We got to know Aboriginal people and appreciate who they were and what they'd been through. Our awareness gradually grew from that to the point where, when things like this come along, I want to contribute. It holds personal significance for me, my family, and for my daughter.

Residential schools were an enormous injustice, and it is a horrific thing to try to destroy a culture. For people like my daughter, the issue was that she was the child of a young Indigenous woman who because of the experience of her parents, really didn't have a home life, a family life that we would consider "normal." Therefore, as a fairly young woman, she was involved in drugs and prostitution.

There was a sense in which her daughter—now my daughter— needed to be rescued from that. This young Indigenous woman went on to have several children who were taken away from her. There's a very real sense in which her life—that is, my daughter's biological mother's life—was destroyed by having her babies seized by the state. She never recovered.

THEY WERE THERE, AND DID THEIR BEST

Patricia Holbrow
Reunion Volunteer and Neighbourhood Resident

Transcribed from an oral interview.

I taught at Kelvin High School. I started there in 1971. I recall that in my first year of teaching, which was 1971–72, we had a number of Aboriginal students at the school. I know at least two who were living with foster families. I don't think they had a legal fostering, but they had come to the city to be able to attend high school, and they were in grade ten.

I also recall there were at least two students I taught who were living at Assiniboia in the residential school.

I don't remember a whole lot. This is forty-five years ago, but I do remember their names and I've thought of them a number of times since then and wondered how things went for them. In those days, you went to your local high school, and that's why they would be coming to Kelvin from the residential school. If they were going to a public school, it would probably be Kelvin, because it was the closest one.

I have often thought, "I wonder how they felt about being there?" There was a boy and a girl. They stuck to themselves a lot, and I think they must have felt a bit out of place because Kelvin primarily housed an upper-middle-class kind of population in those days. I don't remember them mixing, but it was just the way it was. I don't know that anybody really thought about trying to make sure they felt comfortable at Kelvin. They had each other, and that was thought to be fine. There were other students who were living in foster homes who they would associate with, as well. But they were there, and did their best.

Because it was my first year teaching, I was really feeling my way. I got the job in November. School was already in full swing by that time, and I had never taught before. This is one of the reasons that things stand out in my mind.

I remember that the students from Assiniboia were struggling. I wanted to do an awards program for students at the end of the year. There were awards programs for the entire school body, but I just thought, "I wonder what I could do that would be a little bit different?"—and to recognize some students who were not going to be the top students or scholarship winners.

I decided for this grade ten general business class—I taught three or four of them—that I would buy some posters to award to the students who had improved the most over the year. It was my first year, I didn't have a lot of money. I was just out of school myself.

When I started, these particular students were not doing so well; but they improved the most. I remember the other students in the class were so happy these children received the awards, and they were just posters.

They must have been pleased. They had shown remarkable improvement from when I got them in November. And I'm not taking credit for that, but they had a long way to go, so it was easy for them to be the ones who showed the most improvement.

I knew about residential schools because we would hear about them through church, so it was not strange for me to know about them; but I did not know until I started teaching that there was one in the city. I drove by here and would see the sign. But it didn't really click until I started teaching that November, and—oh my goodness— we had students at Kelvin who had come from Assiniboia.

I remember thinking, "This must be very strange for them." I didn't even realize that students would be coming from Assiniboia to a public school. Before, I drove by Assiniboia and thought it was self-contained. I can't say that I ever had a conversation with these students to find out how they felt about it. I just remember them sitting near the back of class, or near a corner. They stuck pretty closely to each other, and understandably so. The rest of the students—a lot of them—had gone to elementary school and all the way through school together. It was a pretty stable neighbourhood, so there wasn't a lot of transiency in those days.

I've often wondered how they made out—what happened to them after grade ten. I was at Kelvin for thirteen or fourteen years, but I don't remember what happened to them beyond grade ten.

There's so much negativity in the press about the terrible things, the tragedies, and, I'm certainly not discounting that in any way. I'm just hoping that there were some of them who had a good or a better experience than is being reported in the press—not to trivialize that at all. A lot of children had a horrific time, and the fact that they were taken away from their families and everything. It's a public shame and we were part of that.

What consoles me a little bit is that I might have had some effect on improving their experience at Kelvin. If my little posters and I played any small role in helping them out, if it made them feel that they had accomplished something and were being recognized and given some sort of a reward—and it was just done within the classrooms; I did them for all of my classes that year, I had six classes I think, and I just wanted to recognize the top couple and who had shown the most improvement; that was my goal. It's easy for the kids who are doing well to continue to do well, but I think showing improvement is really commendable. It showed me that they really had potential, and that they could go on. I am curious about how they did, how they made out, or whether after that first year they just couldn't take it, or they went home.

I have run into a lot of students over the years. After I left Kelvin, I went to Gordon Bell, and we had Aboriginal students there who were part of the sixties scoop as well, and also students who lived with families (as I said, "boarded" with them). They weren't fostered; they were just boarding, and the families were paid to have them in their homes.

I THINK THEY'RE BOYS FROM THE INDIAN SCHOOL

Morgan Sizeland Fontaine

Reunion Volunteer and Former Neighbourhood Resident

As a child I lived in River Heights on Renfrew Street between Grosvenor and Kingsway, three streets over and two blocks south of the Assiniboia Indian Residential School. I knew there was a school on Academy Road for Indian children as I attended Sir John Franklin elementary school only two blocks away, but I don't think anyone knew much about "the Indian school."

Although right in the midst of our community, it was isolated and well hidden behind big fences. I don't remember any interaction with the other kids who were running around and biking all over. Despite attending elementary, junior high, and high school, all in River Heights, not once did I know anything more about the Assiniboia School.

I remember a winter day when three boys came to the door of our house, two standing back at the end of the sidewalk, while one knocked on the door. I saw them coming, so I called my mom. She opened the door and they asked if they could shovel the sidewalk for us. Each boy had a shovel. My mom asked me if I knew these boys, but I didn't. I remember saying, "I think they're boys from the Indian school." So she told them she'd be happy to have the sidewalk shovelled, and when they finished, she gave them some money and hot chocolate.

In talking to others from that era in River Heights, I find that most of us share vague notions about this community history and about the Indigenous people in our midst, but nobody knew much about it at the time.

Twenty years later—to the same month—I started a job with the Department of Indian Affairs. I worked in an office near the boardroom where the meetings with First Nations chiefs were held. Within the first two weeks, a man stopped at my office door and said, "You must be new here. I haven't met you before." We introduced

Figure 58. Winter Carnival on Assiniboia playing field, c. 1964.

ourselves. He was Chief Theodore (Ted) Fontaine of Sagkeeng First Nation. I vividly remember thinking, "I don't know if I've ever met an Indian person before I started this job. What am I doing working here?"

Obviously, the same thought crossed his mind. He asked, "Have you ever been to an Indian reserve?" I had to say no. He very nicely told me, "Well, that's something that would be really good to do. Why don't you come out to Sagkeeng and I'll show you around?"

I agreed that it was a good idea, but didn't know if I would be allowed to do so. And he said, "Oh, don't worry about that." Then he immediately set a date—the Tuesday after the long weekend. "Just come at ten o'clock and meet me at the band office," he said.

I didn't know anything. I was so green. I didn't know where Sagkeeng was or how I would get there. I went to see my boss. He simply said this was a great opportunity. "Get yourself a map and go for the day. You'll learn a lot."

So I did. I took a map and my car and headed out Tuesday morning. I'd never driven on the highway before by myself. It took me almost two hours to get to Sagkeeng from River Heights because I was rechecking my map so often. I got to the band office, and—well there's another whole story about that—but Chief Fontaine showed me around the community.

I learned so much that day, the beginning of a steep learning curve about the true history of Canada, the First Nations of Canada, cross-cultural respect, and most importantly about the deplorable state of my own ignorance. The Chief was very kind and generous in explaining everything. He took me to see the conditions of the homes and roads, the lagoon, school, and the dump. The needs in this community were obvious even to me, a guest who knew nothing.

I remember being invited into the home of Elder Dora Twoheart. The house was terribly dilapidated despite being scrupulously clean. She desperately needed a new house, as did so many. The living conditions in the community were very poor. We spent most of the day driving from place to place, seeing everything up close, with me realizing for the first time the potential purpose and promise of the job and department I worked for.

At the time of my job interview, in 1971, I was told that our mission was to fully support Indian self-government, to work ourselves out of our jobs, that there would be no government bureaucracy in the future lives of First Nations people. I had already committed myself to work in support of this goal. Now I began to understand what it meant.

Over the following years, I had the opportunity to work with Chief Fontaine on a number of federal–First Nations initiatives. A friendship developed that years later became a marriage. We visited both the Fort Alexander and Assiniboia Indian residential school sites many times together and still do.

One day, he started telling me about his experiences in River Heights and the little freedom he enjoyed being out snow shovelling. He was surprised when I told him my memory of those Indian boys coming to shovel. We talked more about those days, and he said that it was him, Teddy and Joe Guy who came to my house. Only the older boys were allowed to go, and a boundary had been set to limit how far they could go. They, of course, had gone beyond the boundary to explore.

We walked from the Assiniboia site to my first home on Renfrew Street and both savoured that sweet memory as if it was yesterday. That house still looks very much as it did then, well-maintained, with a lovely varnished wood front door that my dad made out on our lawn all those years ago. A door that still has the distinctive diamond-shaped window that I remember my dad cutting out to install the glass.

We knew then that our relationship began at that door and that destiny had brought us together again in another doorway twenty years later. Our family, our work, love, and spirituality are our cornerstones. My husband and my dad shared a very special and loving relationship, and my dad was delighted with the Renfrew Street memory of our beginning a life together.

I have a bond with the Assiniboia School that arises from this early connection. We still visit the site frequently. We live nearby, and as we're driving home from somewhere, Theodore will say, "Do you mind if we stop for a few minutes?" And I always say, "Let's."

We come around the building and park at the back overlooking the big green space which was the playing fields for baseball and hockey. Theodore tells me that after enduring ten terrible years of incarceration at the Fort Alexander Indian Residential School, the Assiniboia School was a relief from oppression, near starvation, loneliness, and abuse. To be well-fed, treated with dignity, and allowed to come outside into this big field gave him a freedom that he had not had since before he was seven years old.

We had been together many years before I started to understand these experiences. He began writing about them and eventually asked if I would type them up for him. He was considering submitting one small story for publication. As I started inputting his handwritten pages on the computer, his true story was revealed. It was shocking, heartbreaking, endearing, yet ultimately hopeful. This is how I learned about the reality of Indian residential schools.

That small story was later placed as the first chapter in Theodore's memoir, *Broken Circle, The Dark Legacy of Indian Residential Schools.* Published in 2010, his book is a Canadian national bestseller, used widely in schools, universities, organizations, and corporations across Canada. Publication of *Broken Circle* has unexpectedly led him to speak publicly about his experiences. Every talk, with more than 1,000 to date, leads not only to questions but to revelations, insights, and deeper understanding for both of us. These presentations are always hard, yet incredibly rewarding in shining a bright light on such a dark place of Canada's history.

On the Assiniboia playing fields, I can see Theodore trying to shed some of the trauma of his residential school experiences, to reconnect with the spirits of the other children who became his family, to rediscover his true inner self, the child he was before school, the one he was meant to be.

And, for me, it is also a rediscovery. I can visualize those kids streaming out onto the grass or the snow, escaping the confines of buildings and authority. Out here, I'm at the baseball field, I see the hockey rinks the kids built, I see them flying across the ice at breakneck speed, I see them out here skating really early in the morning before school. I see that through his eyes. I can imagine it, and understand by listening to his stories the depth of his emotions and the life-saving freedom he found on these fields.

We've had the joy of building close relationships with people here at the Canadian Centre for Child Protection. The first time when I went inside with Theodore, he told them that whenever we drive by we stop on the grassy edge of the fields. It became kind of a humorous conversation with them saying, "Oh, we know. We always look out the windows and see you there."

They treasure the fact that he comes here, and we are all conscious of the irony that this is now a centre for child protection. He loves sitting down with them to talk. They've asked him to talk about Indian residential schools and the impact of those experiences on First Nations children and families, impacts they witness firsthand in their work in child protection. They share a very special relationship and invite him here often. This is a treasured relationship for him, significant in his reconciliation process, and very loving.

Theodore talked for a long time about having a reunion at Assiniboia, and because he was in the first class, the 1958–59 year when it opened, his vision of a reunion focused on the people who were in that first class of this first high school for First Nations students in an urban environment. It would be an opportunity for the Survivors to share their stories and memories.

It is hard for me to hear that there were cruel and discriminatory behaviours by people from outside, whether they were River Heights residents or not. They taunted the kids when the students were inside the building. Under the cover of darkness, there would be racist names and so-called "war whoops" yelled out from the safety of Academy Road. The fact that the Survivors still talk about it is a testament to how hurtful those behaviours were. Those white teenagers may have thought it was funny, but it was mean-spirited, such a reflection of ignorance, racism and hatred of kids because they were Indian.

One of Theodore's treasures is the original 1958–59 class photo that used to hang in the original school building. It is a large framed picture that has individual face photos of all the students, each one carefully clipped in place with those little stick-on corners used to mount photos, and in the centre there is a picture of the school and principal Father Robidoux.

Theodore salvaged the picture from the garbage when they were tearing down the school building and gutting it to get rid of everything. At the time, he was visiting from the Northwest Territories and wanted to revisit Assiniboia. He saw the demolition going on, went inside and found a big heap of school artifacts on the floor. The big picture frame was damaged, the glass broken, and the picture hanging out. He was shocked to recognize this as the historic picture of the first class of Assiniboia students. He picked it up and had it restored to its original condition. This is one of his prized treasures. It tells me that these classmates were his family.

He used to keep a smaller reproduction of it on a panel in front of his desk at home. I would often see him looking at it, remembering and wondering what had happened to some of them. Many passed away early in life. He says that fewer than a third may still be alive.

In 2013, Theodore and a few others started calling up some friends from that first Assiniboia class, and from subsequent years of students. A date was set for an informal reunion on the open grass playing fields. The RCMP building was operational then. The RCMP put up their big tipi and allowed the group the use of it for the reunion event.

Quite a number of people came for that reunion, mostly Survivors and their family members, but also River Heights residents. It was very informal, simply a time for gathering and sharing, reminiscing and laughing. It poured rain, torrential rain, all day. We sheltered in the tipis, sharing hot tea, soup, and bannock.

One of the Survivors said, "The heavens are crying on us and on this land. The spirit world is crying on us because of the pain we carry, the students who are gone, the family relationships lost, the communities damaged, the languages forgotten. It's perfectly right that the rain is cleansing us and this land here today."

The reunion was a really good time for sharing and reflection, very sombre in one way but also full of humour. The Survivors were thoughtful, reflective, and profound, the emotions overwhelming, yet the former classmates would be laughing together two seconds later. Through their generosity of spirit, they allowed others like me and visitors from River Heights to experience their stories, adaptability, and enduring resilience.

A second reunion was held in September 2015, with extensive support from the Canadian Centre for Child Protection, the RCMP, and Andrew Woolford and his team. It was a bright and sunny day on the playing fields. The RCMP tipi was again erected, and a microphone with speakers installed on the little rise of land leading up to the road, a natural stage. Survivors and more family members and community residents attended, joined by special guests Father Laurent Alarie, former teacher, and Sister Jean Ell, former head cook. Both were warmly welcomed and remembered by the Survivors, leading to many shared stories about the good food enjoyed at Assiniboia. That day the wind blew strongly all afternoon, sweeping away tears as laughter rose to the heavens.

In June 2017, the third Assiniboia reunion was conducted with support from the Canadian Centre for Child Protection, River Heights faith communities, the University of Manitoba, and many volunteers. The grounds and the former classrooms building were filled with Survivors and guests, with staff of the Canadian Centre for Child Protection providing tours of the building alongside the Survivors sharing their memories. The generosity of Westworth United Church, other churches, and community residents was simply uplifting. Volunteers offered tribute by way of a beautiful tea in the late afternoon for Survivors and family members. A community feast and celebration followed, with speakers, entertainment, and shared food.

It was an outpouring of love and understanding. Every decision was made with thoughtful loving care, symbolic and respectful of First Nations culture and languages, spirituality, and community. Even the bannock was made in the shape of big turtles. Every gesture was a powerful sign of reconciliation, not only in words, but by intention, in actions, in grace. When the Survivors, families, and community members shared this feast, it was a family sharing a meal.

When we sit by the Assiniboia playing fields, I imagine how it was at the best of times—children running, laughing, playing. There is still a chance for this small piece of land to be preserved for children and for Survivors, close to the loving presence of the Canadian Centre for Child Protection. The spirits of those who have died would mingle joyously, reunited with those still living. The sun would shine that day and all their days to come. The circle would be complete.

Figure 59. Harvest Bakery turtle bread, 2017.

PART VI
THE CITY OF WINNIPEG REMEMBERS

Thanks largely to the efforts of Assiniboia Survivors, Winnipeg is beginning to learn about the city's Indian residential school. This has been a slow process, but the determination of Survivors to commemorate their school has registered with the media, the municipal government, churches, schools, as well as other organizations and local businesses. The municipal government is currently working with the Assiniboia Indian Residential School Legacy Group to ensure preservation of the school buildings and fields as a site of memory. Historical Buildings Officer Murray Peterson has been a consistent source of support, information, and humour as the group continues its journey. His efforts to create a City of Winnipeg commemorative display about Assiniboia are included below, as well as an article from the **Winnipeg Free Press.**

ASSINIBOIA RESIDENTIAL SCHOOL INTERPRETIVE PANEL PROJECT

Murray Peterson

Historical Buildings Officer, City of Winnipeg

In August 1997, I wrote a report for the City of Winnipeg's Historical Buildings Committee on the former Julia Clark School, 611 Academy Road. The report, which included one sentence on the building's use as an Indian residential school, dealt mainly with the actual building and was used to evaluate and designate the building as a protected heritage structure.

In May 2016, I attended a meeting discussing possible projects for the City of Winnipeg's Year of Reconciliation. The city was also formalizing its response to "Calls to Action" No. 57, "Professional Development and Training for Public Servants," and wished to include an historical piece on the Assiniboia Indian Residential School. Since I had written a report on the school building, I was asked for my opinion.

The first thought was to mount an exhibition of captioned images of the school to describe its history. My initial research, however, uncovered "happy smiling images" of student lounging on the grounds or reading books. These images did not seem to be telling a complete story nor did they agree with my modest understanding of these types of institutions. I asked for and was given some extra time to gather more information to make a more informed decision on the direction, scope, and content of the display. In the end, my research—scribbled notes, photocopied reports, books, magazines, website information and the like—takes up a fairly large box. This work was necessary to give me a clearer picture of the history of Indian residential schools and how and why they came to be, not just in Winnipeg but across the country. It is a complex story, but this research prepared me for the most important part of the project—listening.

This story is an intensely personal one. If you were to ask the twenty people in my graduating class what they thought of their high-school years, you would not get two answers the same—it was great for some, terrible for others, and some are indifferent to those years. So when asked this same question, the residential school attendees offered similarly different takes. The key was to find balance—something, coincidentally, many of the Survivors say they are doing in their own lives.

What stood out, as I listened to more and more of the stories, were some constants: the stories of loneliness, the isolation they felt from their own culture and the Winnipeg culture in which they were placed, bullying, and physical abuse. There were also success stories: the development of friendships with other students, gaining skills, and athletic performances by individuals and teams.

At the same time as I was collecting research and listening to stories, the project itself was evolving. It was obvious that the finished result was going to be much different than first planned. Members of the city's Indigenous Relations Division, graphic designer Aniko Szabo, the Indigenous Exhibits Working Group, Library Services, and others provided valuable input into how and where it would be most appropriate to display the information.

In the end, an unusual decision was made. With the goal to reach as many people as possible both within the city's workforce and the public-at-large, two sets of interpretive panels were created. One set was housed initially at the Millennium Library and then sent out to be displayed at the city's many neighbourhood libraries. The other set, redesigned as larger banners, were initially set up in the foyer of the Susan A. Thompson Building at City Hall. After several weeks there, they have been hosted by a number of city departments, placed in lobbies and other public spaces accessed by both citizens and employees. The story, told on nine panels, will continue to journey throughout the city.

It is my hope that people reading the panels will get a sense of the horror of Indian residential schools. Beyond that, I would like them to also feel some hope for the future. These Survivors continue to make a positive difference in their communities and in the larger, non-Indigenous community. And, hopefully, empathy for our Indigenous population can come from a better understanding of this past.

This project could not have happened without the dedication and courage of the Survivors. They were so trusting. I sat across tables from them at coffee shops and restaurants, and they told me their most deeply personal stories without hesitation. They placed a great deal of faith in me to listen carefully and tell the truth. I promised them that the final story would be theirs and theirs alone—the Survivors had the final say in how the panels looked and what information was on them. It was a group effort, as panels like this usually are.

Many of the Survivors talk about their "journey," and when I look back on this project, I realize it was a journey for me as well. I learned about forgiveness. I learned about trust and strength and compassion by talking to the Survivors and seeing how they have lived their lives. That they have been able to move beyond their past, to find themselves again, and to share and teach others is the true gift for all of us. Understanding their story and witnessing their ability to triumph makes us all better people.

The kindness and patience shown me by these people was remarkable. I treasure the friendships I have made because of this project.

Assiniboia Survivor Theodore Fontaine congratulated me one time for all the work on the project, and I started into my usual speech about all the help and support I had received.

He interrupted me and said, "Murray, just say 'Thank you.'"

Following this page: Figures 60 to 67. Information panels from City of Winnipeg Assiniboia display.

ASSINIBOIA RESIDENTIAL SCHOOL

621 Academy Road
Winnipeg Manitoba

Picture a busy high school with students going back and forth from their classroom to their residence. In the winter, there were hockey rinks and in the summer, baseball diamonds. This was how the school looked to the outside world.

Winnipeg's Assiniboia Indian Residential School operated from 1958 to 1973.

Know there was a different reality experienced by the students who were being systematically assimilated.

Recognize how difficult life was for these students from Indian Reserves all over Manitoba, Saskatchewan, Northwest Ontario and other Canadian provinces.

Imagine how alone they felt, struggling in a strange place with no family support, traditional culture or familiar language.

Admire the strength of graduates who flourished as professionals – engineers, lawyers, doctors, nurses, teachers, artists, leaders and healers.

It is a legacy of fear and triumph, self-doubt and resiliency.

Celebrate those who found themselves.

Remember the children and adults who were lost.

Support those students and their families who are still trying to find their way.

WE WERE THERE

These are the first residents of Assiniboia Residential School.

The incarceration of these children is finally being recognized for its lifelong damage. However, as of 2017, less than half of this class has lived to be part of this acknowledgment.

Many of these students were not provided with transportation home and were forced to remain over the extended Christmas holidays and during the summer. Although students suffered, rules slowly began to relax, making life at the school easier for those who followed.

SCHOOL IN THE BIG CITY

Early students at Assiniboia Residential School were completely cut off from their families and community, their River Heights neighbours, and from the larger Winnipeg society.

Teenagers experienced feelings of loneliness and detachment during their stay at Assiniboia.

This slowly changed. Sporting teams were allowed to participate in games, then tournaments, then leagues. Students were taken for downtown shopping trips and entered work-experience programs. After 1967, students attended classes in area high schools.

These difficult experiences forged closer bonds among the students.

ASSINIBOIA RESIDENTIAL SCHOOL 621 ACADEMY RD

GOVERNMENT EDUCATIONAL SYSTEM

"Indian children should be withdrawn as much as possible from the parental influence."

— Prime Minister Sir John A. Macdonald,
Identify describing the intention of the system, 1879

Winnipeg's Assiniboia Residential School was part of the federal government's educational system under the Indian Act based on the objective of assimilation to destroy the students' culture, language and identity and to urbanize these young adults.

"A spruce tree taken while young from a low lying moist soil when transplanted into light soil dies in most cases.
If it lives, it will be but short and stunted, where it would have been tall and straight had it been left in its natural soil.
It will be like this despite the greatest of care.
It is not because it has no capacity for growth, it is because it is taken out of its natural environment where it would have done well."

— Chief Poundmaker,
describing the effects of Canada's residential school system, 1931

"We should never forget, even once they have learned from it, because it's part of who we are.
It's not just a part of who we are as survivors and children of survivors and relatives of survivors, it's part of who we are as a nation.
And this nation must never forget what it once did to its most vulnerable people."

— Senator Murray Sinclair,
Chief Commissioner of the Truth and Reconciliation Commission, 2017

"Like me, most survivors waited a decade or more before going back to school. Some went back even 15, 20 or 25 years later to study the things that as children they'd dreamed of studying – law, medicine, education, etc.
But Canada lost many great contributions from its First Nations citizens because of the residential schools system."

— Theodore Fontaine,
Assiniboia Residential School Survivor, 2017

WHY THIS DISPLAY?

The City of Winnipeg declared 2016 its Year of Reconciliation.

Led by its Indigenous Relations Division, documents and stories continue to be identified and shared by its Archives and Library.

These panels represent just one way the City of Winnipeg is responding the Truth and Reconciliation Commission (TRC) Calls to Action.

The TRC was established in June 2008 as part of the 2007 Indian Residential Schools Settlement Agreement. After six years travelling across Canada and listening to more than 6,500 witnesses, the Commission found:

- Canada's Indian Residential School System operated between 1883 and 1996 with over 150,000 First Nations, Métis and Inuit children placed in schools across the country.

- The odds of a student dying while in the system were higher than the odds for Canadians serving in the Second World War.

It is estimated that over 6,000 children died at Residential schools in Canada.

Truth and Reconciliation Commission of Canada: Calls to Action

MAYOR'S DECLARATION

THE YEAR OF RECONCILIATION

"Reconciliation must inspire Aboriginal and non-Aboriginal peoples to transform Canadian society so that our children and grandchildren can live together in dignity, peace, and prosperity on these lands we now share."

–Final Report of the *Truth and Reconciliation Commission of Canada* [2015]

ACKNOWLEDGEMENTS

This project could not have been possible without the support of the following:

Andrew Woolford, University of Manitoba
Archives of Manitoba

City of Winnipeg staff in:
• City Services
• Indigenous Relations Division
• Planning, Property and Development Department
• Winnipeg Public Library
Library and Archives Canada

Sinnott Centre for Truth and Reconciliation

Manitoba Film Space's Education Resource Centre Inc.

Financial support from the Social Sciences and Humanities Research Council of Canada through the Manitoba Research Alliance and the City of Winnipeg's Gail Asper Memorial Fund

Assiniboia Residential School Survivors and the Survivors Gathering Council

The oldest and largest Exhibits

Photography captured with permission of C. Kavanagh, D. Brophy, F. & M. Sorensen, Manitoba Society Hall of Fame, Assiniboia Residential School Survivors' Gathering Council

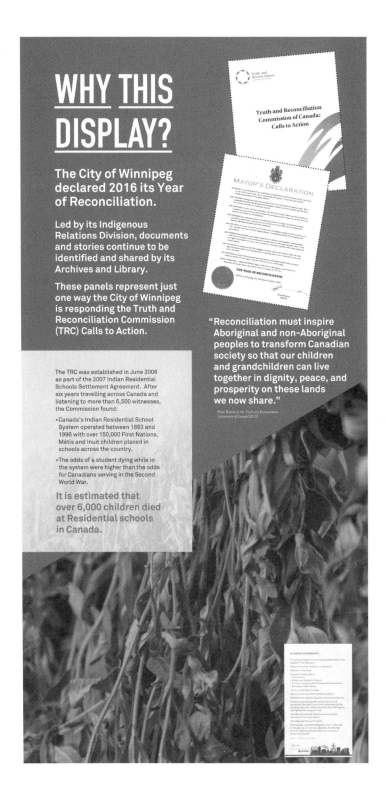

THE INSTITUTION

Assiniboine Residential school operated as a high school from September 1958 to 1967 and a hostel from 1967 to 1973 and was attended by more than 600 students.

The school was federally funded and operated by the Oblate Fathers of Mary Immaculate and the Grey Nuns. Students ranged in age from 15 to 20 with yearly enrolment averaging 100.

The school is now the Canadian Centre for Child Protection.

- First group of students organized into four classes, Grades 8 to 10 (Grade 12 added in September 1960).

- In 1967 school became a hostel, with students living in the dormitories and attending classes at schools like St. Charles Academy, Daniel McIntyre Collegiate (Selkirk, MB), R.B. Russell, Gordon Bell, Earl Grey, J.B. Mitchell, Silver Heights, Grant Park, St. Mary's Academy and Kelvin High School.

- Special programming included Cadet Corps, sports teams that competed in regional tournaments, choirs, etc.

- Location was opened in 1915 as an abandoned and abused children's home and in the 1940s and 1950s was used as a veterans' convalescent hospital.

- A portion of the former school site was acquired by the City of Winnipeg in 1976 and the dormitory buildings were demolished a decade later. The school building (opened in 1918) and gymnasium/chapel (opened in 1966) remain standing today.

Srs Grises de Montréal
Maison Mère
Arch...

INDIAN ☩ THE MISSIONARY RECORD

OTTAWA, CANADA

JAI-53-R-3546
RGE. N.A. LACHANCE
MAISON DES GRISES
1190 RUE GUY
MONTREAL 25 P.Q.

NOVEMBER, 1952

VOL. XV, NO. 9

TRAINING LEADERS WILL SAVE INDIAN RACE — Will Encourage Indians to Return to Reserves.

Oblate Commission Plans Indian High Schools

OTTAWA. — By far the more widespread missionary organization in Canada is that of the Missionary Oblates of Mary Immaculate, whose interest in missionary work among Canada's 135,000 Indians and 9,000 Eskimos has been maintained for over 100 years.

The activities of the Oblates in recent years have been extended to the point where they now maintain 199 mission posts, 41 residential schools, 15 hospitals, 115 Indian and 26 Eskimo missions.

Nearly 400 Oblate Fathers, 100 Lay Brothers, over 400 Sisters of various congregations and numerous lay teachers compose the personnel of the missions which are grouped into 8 Vicariates Apostolic and 4 regional Provinces.

A special organization called "the Indian and Eskimo Welfare Commission," the membership of which embraces all the Vicars Apostolic and the Provincials, meets every year in Ottawa to review the missionary activities and to decide upon future policies.

ELECTIONS OF OFFICERS

Most Reverend H. Routhier, O.M.I., Vic-Apostolic Coadjutor of Grouard, Alberta, has been elected president, the Vice-Presidents are the Most Reverend Anthony Jordan, O.M.I. (Prince Rupert, B.C.) and M. Lajeunesse, O.M.I. (Keewatin, Man.); counsellors are the Very Reverend S. A. Larochelle, O.M.I. (Montreal) and J. R. Birch, O.M.I. (Ottawa) who is also the Treasurer.

The General Superintendent of the Commission is Rev. André Renaud, O.M.I., B.A., L.Ph., L.Th., the General Secretary and Director of the Division of Public Relations is Rev. G. Laviolette, O.M.I.

FOR HIGHER EDUCATION

This year's meeting of the Commission was deemed one of the most important by virtue of the decisions taken, which involve a reversal of the traditional policy in education for the Indians.

The present school curriculum, is to be extended on a far-reaching plan, to embrace a system of ... tion for Indian stud... ...cation ... resolved to

NEW HOSPITAL AT SMITH
By BERNARD BROWN, O.M.I.

The biggest building north of Edmonton, Alberta, is now under construction. It is the new General Hospital at the Oblate Mission Center at Fort Smith, N.W.T. From end to end, inside and out, it is being put up by Oblate Missionary Lay Brothers.

The brothers not only drew up the blueprints for the hospital but they made the lumber at their own sawmill from logs that they themselves cut. They are competently manning all the construction jobs that go with the building in the sub-Arctic. They are running up a large, three-decker, massive, chimney; they are installing electrical dumb-waiters; they are welding together an elaborate system of high-pressure steam heating.

They are doing all this in addition to such run-of-the-mill jobs as hanging 165 big hospital doors, digging drainage ditches and putting up partitions.

The statistics involved in the new mission hospital would be impressive anywhere, even down "in civilization." But up in the North West Territories, they are staggering. The building itself is laid out in the form of a "T", 121 by 170 feet. Its three stories contain 33,600 square feet of floor space. Besides regular operating rooms and maternity wards, the hospital will have one (the third) reserved to tubercular patients. The disease is the scourge of the Indians; tuberculosis of the bone whom Eskimos as well, serve.

Existing mission hospitals are Oblates' sub-Arctic jammed already ... ariate are of these corridors with natives ... long-term patients suffering from tuberculosis. Indians and Eskimos seem as yet, built up little to this white man's disease. The new hundred beds tains one ... purposes. The boilers with cord wood (coal is expensive due to transportation costs) cut by the Oblate brothers are part of the big burr. The boilers will burn 5 cords a day during the cold winter. As you account the brothers ting the finishing touches hospital to the bare... Well here ...

Returns to Teach Own People

MISS THERESA MINDE, a member of Ermineskin Indian Band, is the daughter of Mr. and Mrs. Joe Minde. She received her early education at St. Joseph's Convent, Red Deer, Alberta. ... her High School at St. Joseph's Convent, Red Deer Normal School; ...tended University of Alberta ...
... Alberta.

THE SITE PLAN
CIRCA 1960

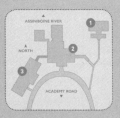

ASSINIBOINE RIVER

NORTH

ACADEMY ROAD

Classroom Building
The building was originally known as the Julia Clark School when it was completed for the Children's Home of Winnipeg in 1918. In 1997, the City of Winnipeg designated it a Historic Building.

Main Building
The boy's Dormitory in 1974. The dining room, with girls on one side and boys on the other, was located on the main floor.

West Wing
The Girl's Dormitory, in 1969. The girls had a long walk to get to their classrooms.

Our School

THE
FUTURE

In June 2017, a Reunion and Commemorative Event was held on the school site.

Left to right: Group of survivors and family members in the sharing/ceremony tent. Group of survivors and neighbours visiting former school building. Survivors at the former school building. Survivors with staff from the Canadian Centre for Child Protection. Tips holding out a light of the school site. Photographs reproduced with permission from The Survivors Committee Council.

More than 250 people, survivors, River Heights neighbours and non-Indigenous Winnipeggers toured the former school building.

Many expressed shock and remorse. They did not know the history of the residential school system in Canada and that there was a residential school in their own community.

Then the neighbours expressed empathy and understanding – part of the process of building meaningful relationships with those who share this community.

Led by survivors and supported by the community...

Plans are being finalized for a permanent marker and remembrance plaza on Academy Road and for the collection and publishing of survivors' experiences.

Figure 68. Dancers perform at the 2017 Assiniboia reunion.

LA VÉRITÉ

Aila Potosky

Children taken from homes
Taken to change them
Erase their roots
Be like the Europeans
Keep away from family at large, cold, heartless schools
Erase their culture
Cut off their hair, be like everyone else, dress like others,
Force language, force religion and beliefs, keep siblings far away
No visits from parents
Learn to follow rules or be punished
Truth kept

Government began to realize the cruel ways
Mistakes had been made
All cultures should be celebrated
To create a unique Canada
A Canada that embraces individuality
Action towards reconciliation needed to happen
Educate new generations
Honour Aboriginal culture and rebuild pride
Truth be told

I imagine a Canada that is . . .
Sharing stories through experiences
Honesty, apologies, a new pride
Canadians embracing all Canadians
Equality and acceptance for all
All cultures are accepted
Everyone is respected
People are proud of who they are
Truth be heard

Miigwetch

Aila Potosky wrote this award-winning poem as a grade five student at École Sun Valley, Winnipeg, February 2019.

CANADIAN CENTRE FOR CHILD PROTECTION

Lianna McDonald, Executive Director

I first met Theodore Fontaine on a cold morning right before Christmas in 2014. One of our staff had found him sitting in his red car in the parking lot. He told us he was a Survivor who attended classes at the Assiniboia Indian Residential School, the building that is now home to the Canadian Centre for Child Protection (C3P). He explained he often parked out back to visit old memories and recall his years at school. We invited him to spend the morning with our team a few weeks later where he generously shared both his time and his memories—the hard ones and the happier ones—to help us better understand the shadowed history of our building and the impacts of residential schools across Canada.

C3P is a national charity dedicated to the personal safety of all children. Every day we work to reduce the sexual abuse and exploitation of children, assist in the location of missing children, and prevent child victimization through a number of programs, services, and resources for Canadian families, educators, child-serving organizations, and law enforcement. Our organization was founded as Child Find Manitoba in 1985, only twelve years after the residential school had shut its doors.

Through Theodore we met the rest of the Assiniboia Legacy Group. In 2015, we hosted a Survivors' reunion on the grounds behind our building to meet many others and to mark the storied history of what took place there. Two years later we opened our doors to both Survivors and the community for a second reunion and tours of the building.

Today we honour the students who sat and learned so many years ago in what is now our office space dedicated to the protection of children. We share the history with visitors, pausing to point out the class photo we have of the first students who attended the school back in 1958. We also welcome the Survivors on the occasions when they come together and meet in our boardrooms to continue their important legacy efforts.

Our agency now works closely with a different population of survivors of child sexual abuse—those whose abuse was recorded and distributed online. We know that there is nothing that better helps the world listen and understand the lifelong impacts of these crimes than the brave voices of Survivors. Their courageous choice in sharing their stories means that we must listen, pay attention, and understand what, for far too long, has been hidden in the dark.

In the same way, we are inspired by the Assiniboia School Survivors, who have found the continued strength and courage to share their voices and stories after everything that they endured. We are thankful to them for revisiting difficult parts of their histories to share their stories with Canadians—an important part of our history that for too long has been hidden, and must be understood both for our history and future.

As a society we must do more to protect children. Our agency will continue to fight every day to make the world a safer place for kids.

RESIDENTIAL SCHOOL IN CITY'S BACKYARD

Catherine Mitchell
Winnipeg Free Press, 30 May 2015

Theodore "Ted" Fontaine stands a little bent. It's his hip. He leans into the well of a big window of his long-ago classroom at the Assiniboia Indian Residential School.

Winnipeggers may not have heard of it. They cannot see it, even though the building stands limestone-sturdy; it's hidden by newer buildings where Academy Road meets Route 90. Through spattering rain, he looks onto the backyards of tidy little houses on Wellington Crescent South. The people who lived there have all likely moved on, says Fontaine, seventy-three.

I wonder if they knew you were here, I say.

"Oh, they knew. They had gardens. We were hungry," he says with a grin.

This is a story of survival and transformation. Yes, reconciliation. It's about chance, fate, and other words used to describe stuff we can't explain.

Nipping tomatoes and cucumbers is one thing Fontaine, a former Sagkeeng chief, remembers of his time in River Heights, at the school where he spent grade ten in 1958, and part of grade eleven before he "walked away" to work in the bush.

It is a classic building, stone with understated ornamentation on the facade, built in 1918 by the Winnipeg School Division for the Children's Home of Winnipeg, which had its boys' and girls' residences on the spot where the RCMP forensic lab now sits.

This is how history hides.

The school itself is now home to the Canadian Centre for Child Protection, the doggedly determined organization that tracks down Internet predators and missing children.

In what was Fontaine's first classroom, cyber-sleuths pore over website links, documenting child pornography and other unholy abuses against tender innocents.

The irony—residential school to child saviour—is not lost on Fontaine, who, after repeat visits to make peace with his past, has made close associations with centre staff.

There are scars. He remembers the taunts of the neighbourhood kids walking past his third-floor dorm window on fall evenings, after the Grey Nuns and Oblate fathers who ran the school from 1958 to 1972 sent them to bed. Fontaine was fifteen in the school's first year.

"You plop a residential school in the middle of River Heights, it wasn't nice. We would go to bed by 9:00 p.m., up here on the third floor and there'd be young people going back and forth doing war whoops and stuff."

Still, compared to his early school years at Fort Alexander Indian Residential School, Assiniboia was "like a breath of fresh air." The director, Father Omer Robidoux, was a gem. "A lot of people think they (residential school staff) were monsters," Fontaine says. "They weren't. We loved him. He was very kind."

Robidoux encouraged the boys, hungry for pocket change to spend at the pharmacy across the road, to shovel driveways for nearby residents. It was the most contact they had with their neighbours, those strangers. And they were occasionally shown small kindnesses.

Like the day he and a couple others took their shovel and landed a gig at the door of one house, nearer Grosvenor Avenue. A young girl answered the door: "Mom, I think they're those Indians from the school." They shovelled, pocketed their coins, and were offered hot chocolate.

Like most things in life, the residential schools story can't be wedged neatly into good and bad, black and white. Lifting the lid off the experiences of former residential school students set off a gusher of horrendous stories, now documented by Canada's Truth and Reconciliation Commission.

Yet to say the obscene abuses, the cultural decimation, happened amid a prevailing evil gives short shrift to how history happens. The federal policy, born of a desire to kill the Indian in the child, was racist, destructive, and self-serving for governments of the day. But the staff who visited ruin upon children worked beside teachers, caretakers, supervisors who nurtured their charges.

Fontaine lived the fuller context. He was beaten at Fort Alex. Taught to look down on his own people, he was scornful of his parents upon returning home in the summer. He says his confidence and self-esteem were trampled by a system designed to erase his identity.

Yet, he found some freedom at Assiniboia, made lasting friendships, with children from across Manitoba.

But he itched to get out.

He figures Winnipeggers didn't know much about the city's only residential school. And there's nothing prominently marking the spot.

Ry Moran[1] wants to change that. The director of the TRC's permanent research centre at the University of Manitoba wants to plant a commemorative plaque on Wellington Crescent near the walking/cycling trail next to the Assiniboine River, opposite a baseball field.

That field was a playground for the Assiniboia children. It was where hockey scouts, like Joe Mendella, local man for the Detroit Red Wings, would spy prospects on the rink there. Mendella signed Fontaine to a "C contract," that sent the young man to camp in Flin Flon. He didn't stay.

What followed were the lost years, when he hit the bottle. Fontaine always worked, but he would not find his way until his thirties, when he graduated from civil engineering at the Northern Alberta Institute of Technology. He had a successful career in mineral exploration before working for the lands division of Indian Affairs.

Fontaine succeeded in life. But he wonders how much he might have done, what all the children might have done, if their lives weren't moulded by a failed policy to assimilate.

He met his future wife, who also worked at Indian Affairs, thirty-three years ago. For the second time, as it turned out.

She was the young thing at the door of that River Heights house twenty years earlier, who called her mom when the "Indian" boys turned up looking to make some spending money.

His wife, Morgan, is helping Fontaine document his journey. He has done some 300 speaking engagements, published his first book *(Broken Circle: The Dark Legacy of Indian Residential Schools)*, reunited with friends from Assiniboia.

It's part of a long, hard slog to make peace with a piece of Canada's past, to resolve the mutual racism, distrust, and resentments infecting our communities. Misunderstanding. The residential school policy happened to all of us, we agree.

In the end, we're all just walking each other home, I say, ripping off of a bit of wisdom from Richard Alpert, better known as Ram Dass.

"I like that," Fontaine nods. His analogy is the ladder: Tall and steep, those who climb out must remember not to pull it up after them, but leave it in place for the others who follow.

Or maybe, more fitting for Winnipeg, we're still clearing driveways after the storm, to reach our neighbours' doors.

PART VII
REUNION, REMEMBRANCE, AND RECLAMATION

Up to this point, the reader will have encountered the Assiniboia reunion several times. There were, in fact, three reunions. The first was organized by the Survivors and was held in 2013. The second, in 2015, was organized by the same Survivors with support of the Canadian Centre for Child Protection. The third, where much of the knowledge for this book was gathered, occurred in June 2017. The third reunion brought together approximately 300 people, a larger event, reaching more Assiniboia Survivors than the previous ones. It also drew more upon community resources, enlisting churches, schools, local businesses, local government, and other groups in helping the Survivors celebrate and remember their time at Assiniboia. The next two pieces reflect on the 2017 reunion, both as a knowledge-gathering event and a reclamation of the former school site as a place of commemoration, where the presence of the Survivors will be given permanence

REUNION AND REMEMBRANCE:
GATHERING KNOWLEDGE

Andrew Woolford

It was only halfway through the reunion that I stopped using the word "research." We were at the former school site at sunrise when I realized my error. In the pipe ceremony, we formed a circle. Most spoke on their thoughts about the reunion—the pain, hope, and possibilities of healing. But one of the participants wondered, "We have been debating whether we are just being researched again." I recognized my oversight. The previous day, I had spoken of "research funds" having supported the event. But I was also well aware that, as Linda T. Smith states, "research" is a dirty word for Indigenous peoples, who have had their cultures invaded and knowledge extracted.[1] In practice, I had not been conducting research during this event—our goal was to open a space for knowledge sharing, in the Survivor's own voice, rather than for the extraction of data. Those collecting remembrances were instructed they were not answering a research question or hypothesis through the interviews. Their role was to listen and record, not to direct, interpret, or lead the discussion. Participants were asked to discuss only what they wished to share and nothing more. But the old linguistic habit, a muscle-memory of the tongue, brought "research" out of my mouth.

When it came to my time in the circle, I thought I would speak to this. But as I talked about my journey as a scholar, I came around to my dad, who was at the end of his life, immobilized by multiple system atrophy and slowly dying on a hospital bed in Victoria, British Columbia. As soon as the reunion was done, I would go Victoria to help care for him. The reunion, as a space of reflection and healing, as a space for family, and loss of family, as a deeper embodied knowledge, struck me. I needed to get home. We all need to remember.

THE BEGINNING

I met several members of this project's governing council through another project, where we were working together to render residential school memories within a virtual space.[2] During our conversations, the Survivors mentioned their efforts to advance memory of the Assiniboia Indian Residential School, where they had spent their high-school years. I offered to apply for a small grant to support their efforts. I knew that the Manitoba Research Alliance had at its disposal a pot of research money and that it was committed to Indigenous community-led research strategies. I applied, stating simply that I wanted to consult with a group of Survivors and former students from Assiniboia[3] to find out what research projects they would like to see created around their school. They generously provided the funding, despite the fact that the open-ended nature of the proposed project placed it out-of-step with most funding evaluation protocols. With the funding, the Survivors took it upon themselves to form a Survivor Governing Council to lead our work on Assiniboia.

Despite this initial commitment to community-led research, the project nonetheless was framed as research. The funds were research funds, and the Assiniboia group was to be consulted to direct research. Research outputs would be expected to support future grants and to demonstrate productivity. We were squarely within the knowledge regime of the university.

At our first meeting, however, this regime was immediately challenged. After a smudge and prayer, as well as some initial steps towards getting to know one another and building trust, the discussion was opened for the former Assiniboia students and Survivors to provide direction. But typical academic outputs were not their primary concern. The first speaker mentioned that they, as a group, did not know enough about who is still alive and who is no longer with us, and that gathering this information would be important. She and another Survivor then suggested that a large reunion be held. Smaller ones had taken place previously through the efforts of Survivors, with the assistance of the Canadian Centre for Child

Protection, who currently lease the former Assiniboia classrooms building, as well as a few other volunteers. But it was hoped that the current project would be able to reach out to more former Assiniboia students.

The next speaker mentioned how there is so little knowledge about Assiniboia—in Winnipeg, but also across Canada. Assiniboia, he felt, was a very distinct place. The survival of the building in which their classes were held, as well as the fields on which they played sports and spent their free time, made it imperative that efforts be made to preserve the site. He wanted us to work toward designing and erecting on the site a commemorative marker and educational display about the school.

It was only with the third speaker that we came to a more traditional academic output—a book. But the book was not envisioned as research; rather, it was viewed as the accumulated *knowledge* of the Survivors and former students. At a later session, after my first attempt to draft an outline for this book according to what I envisioned as the key themes, the Survivors and former students gave direction on how the book should be organized by the different eras that attended, noting that there existed distinct experiences of Assiniboia depending on when one was at the school. This was not data to be organized, coded, and analyzed by me as the researcher. Their stories would carry the book, along with any images we could find to illustrate their remembrances. I was asked to help edit the book, which I have attempted to do with a light hand and a great deal of support from all of the people listed within these pages, though any errors or oversights are mine.

With respect to all three of the Survivor Governing Council's goals, our efforts are not best described as research, at least in a European sense. Though information has been gathered, this information is better understood as knowledge intended to benefit the community and to ensure the preservation of history. The outcome of our collective effort is a gathering of experiences and not a set of hypotheses to be tested through evaluation of evidence. It is "research as ceremony" in that it is based on accountable relationships to one another, but also to the knowledge itself, with full recognition that the Survivors have ownership and control of the stories.[4]

EXTRACTION, DISPOSSESSION, ERASURE

The negative connotations of the word "research" are based on the experiences of Indigenous people with academic researchers. Too often, Indigenous knowledge is extracted from Indigenous peoples, leaving them dispossessed and erased from the discussion, paralleling the dispossession and erasure that colonialism has imposed on Indigenous territories. Through knowledge extraction, ideas shared in conversation become the sole possession of the researcher, translated into an arcane language that is no longer accessible to the community. The knowledge becomes a resource used for individual gain—for example, publication, promotion, and reputation—with little to no benefit to the community. This approach to academic research has been roundly criticized by Indigenous scholars, leaders, and many others.[5] Decolonizing and Indigenous research practices have grown in response. Though I have read and engaged with this research, I do not pretend to fully inhabit such an approach. For one, many of the Indigenous research approaches assume grounding in an Indigenous ontology, or world view, something that I, as a settler Canadian, cannot claim.[6] My experience is imbued with the practices and habits of settler discourses, institutions, and ways of seeing and being in the world. I am engaged in a continuing project to unsettle this heritage, but I am not there yet. Because of this, and following in the footsteps of Paulette Regan, I tend to describe my approach as an unsettling methodology.[7]

My background studying settler colonial institutions and power made me increasingly aware of how little impact my research was having on the everyday lives of those with whom I was most concerned. In earlier work, I had shown how residential schools were part of a larger pattern of settler colonial genocide implemented through multiple auspices, institutions, organizations, and local actors in North America.[8] Through this project, I had sought to serve as a public scholar, speaking out against those who belittled or dismissed Indigenous justice claims. But the world of engaged rhetoric can only take one so far. Minds were sometimes changed, as far as I know, but this was limited, no matter how nuanced my exposition of the problem. Indeed, some arguments I engaged in the media likely appeared little more than a ritualistic debate about genocide and its applicability in a Canadian context. Survivors and Indigenous communities gained too little from this research. It also contributed to a continuation of what Eve Tuck refers to as "damage-based" research.[9] I was inspired by German researchers who had faced their history and sought to show its continuity into the present,[10] but had not yet created adequate space in my work for resilient, community-based partnerships. It may sound as though I am being hard on myself by saying this, but this is not the case. It is an honest critical assessment, recognizing my academic work reached several students and fellow scholars, but remains largely sequestered in an academic context.

In the course of meeting with the Assiniboia Survivors, I was thus presented with a real opportunity to try to use academic resources to respond to the everyday needs of a particular Survivor community.

Of course, I flinched, at least on the inside, when I received my directions from the Survivor Governing Council for our project. I thought, "How am I going to pull off a reunion? I know nothing about doing this sort of thing." As an introvert, most at home at a keyboard in my office, this suggestion went well beyond my comfort zone. But, unsettling oneself means being out of one's comfort zone. Seeking social change through comfortable strategies, indeed, is oxymoronic, if not downright lazy.

Unsettling Methodologies

Unsettling my relationship with knowledge through this project thus entailed surrendering ownership, control, access, and possession to the community with which I was working.[11] To make this possible, an accountable and ongoing relationship was established with the Survivor Governing Council (SGC) to ensure their priorities were also the priorities of the project. Typical academic achievements were not the driving motivation for our efforts, but rather the community needs as the SGC understood them. As well, the SGC's expertise, rather than the expertise of the researcher gleaning knowledge from archive and interviews, was prioritized.[12] Their remembrances, and the wisdom gained through their experience, form the historical and conceptual framework for this project. And through this knowledge, our work endeavours to forge real healing and commemorative opportunities for former students of Assiniboia.

The memories we gather here do not always align, and I do not do the work of trying to organize them into a neat, coherent picture for the reader. They are a multi-vocal and multi-perspectival take on the Assiniboia Indian Residential School. They form not a straightforward or simple narrative, but rather a cyclical and processual knowledge derived from experience.[13]

They are an incomplete set of remembrances. We did not succeed in reaching everyone, and given the early passing of many Assiniboia graduates, we could never reach them all. This is a modest project, both in its smallness and in the modesty demanded by the Survivor Governing Council in going about our work. The Assiniboia reunion was not to be an opportunity for anyone to advance a particular political point of view, or to advance their own career. It was to be an occasion to open ourselves to one another in a spirit of resurgence and relationship.

REUNION AND RECLAMATION

The reunion, as I understood my directions from the Assiniboia Survivor Governing Council, was to serve a dual purpose. Most important was the need to bring Survivors and former students together before too much more time passed and too many more Survivors passed away. As Morgan Fontaine told me after the reunion, "This is about healing, and it is healing that occurs through opening space where new memories can be formed." Many Survivors and former students view their school cohorts as their families, since residential schools did such a viciously effective job of severing them from their families of origin. The reunion had the feel of a family gathering, where memories were recounted, but also out of which new stories took shape.

The other purpose, however, was to reach out to the broader community and raise awareness that Assiniboia had been there, and that its classroom and fields remain as a reminder of Canada's effort to assimilate Indigenous peoples. For the Survivors and former students, there was no sense of contradiction between the fact that many of them had positive experiences at Assiniboia, but also felt a deep loss because of how schools such as Assiniboia sought to disconnect them from their Indigenous heritage. They did not fall into Senator Lynn Beyak's trap,[14] whereby talk of the negative of residential schools is construed to mean there could not be positive moments within a larger, genocidal context. Communicating this complex knowledge to settler Canadians, newcomers, and intergenerational Survivors was a key mission for the project. Parts of the reunion were to be open to the public, bringing Assiniboia to an audience who knew too little about its exceptional existence.

To realize these objectives, the Survivor Governing Council formed partnerships with other community stakeholders, some of which were engaged in their own reconciliation projects, addressing their past complicity in and continuing reproduction of settler colonial power. These included churches, school groups, Indigenous organizations, government, and other parties. Some were asked simply to provide funding, but others were included in a planning committee tasked with organizing a reunion dinner and dance for the Survivors and former students. Many people pulled together to plan a reunion feast. Indeed, I felt a great sense of relief when representatives from the Westworth United Church, St. Andrew's River Heights United Church, the Salvation Army, the Catholic Diocese of Winnipeg, and others agreed to participate on our planning council. The opportunity to avail ourselves of their expertise in organizing public events was invaluable, and the event would not have been as successful without their hard work.

The first event of the reunion was a tour of the school that took place on 23 June 2017. Unfortunately, I had planned poorly for the weather and the number of people who attended. An unseasonably cold and wet late June day brought most of the Survivors and tour seekers inside the tight foyer of the former classrooms building, now occupied by the Canadian Centre for Child Protection (3CP). The 3CP generously offered to stop all other activities from 1:00 p.m. to 4:00 p.m. that afternoon, since the sensitive nature of their work prevents them from continuing their activities when members of the public are present. But as people started to swell into their office space, they began to organize visitors into tour groups, assigning one of their employees to lead each tour. More challenging was my responsibility, finding a Survivor to accompany each tour group so that information about the building's current use, provided by the 3CP staff member, could be accompanied by a former student who would speak a little about their time at the school. But their emotion of re-entering this space, as well as the first reconnection with old friends, made this difficult. Some accompanied the tours, while others mingled. In some cases, I gave tours based on what I had learned about Assiniboia, while Survivors such as Betty Ross and Theodore Fontaine spoke to several groups.

A pair of graduate students and a postdoctoral scholar joined several of the tours and recorded reactions and discussions that took place. Watching these videos now, I can see what valuable interactions were captured on those tapes. We learned much about the classrooms building, what was inside of it, as well as the other buildings on the site that are no longer there. Betty conversed not only with her audience, but with the building itself. It was not only the building in the present; she felt its presence across time, remembering the nuns and fathers who occupied the space; she shared her feelings from various points in time, as well as her thoughts on returning to the space. She presented not a linear narrative, but a story in movement that circulated about the audience, bringing them closer to the power of her magnificent spirit.

Some conversations were more difficult, as was the knowledge they uncovered. At one moment, I accompanied a pair of Survivors to join a group in the building's basement. In the stairwell, one of the two began to experience feelings of panic. She needed to leave. During her time at Assiniboia, the basement housed a dentist's office. She received the knowledge that she had work to do in recovering a memory from this space, but, in the moment, it was overwhelming and she could not remain. Her friend took her aside while I ran to fetch a cultural support worker.

Once the tour was done, Survivors and former students travelled to the nearby Westworth United Church for an afternoon tea prior to the evening's feast. A room was set aside for the Survivors with tea, bannock, and jam from local donors. Other than the members of the various congregations who had volunteered to serve the group, this was a space solely for reconnection and reunion. While they chatted, sipped, and snacked, the rest of the community volunteers worked on decorating and preparing the gymnasium for the dinner.

Figure 69. Reunion tour of the Assiniboia classrooms building, 2017.

The plan to host a community dinner attended by River Heights residents, Assiniboia Survivors, and their families emerged from the SGC. The idea was to sit together and break bread, so that the two communities, separated despite the location of Assiniboia in River Heights, could at last come together. However, as we approached the dinner and confronted the reality that space restrictions would prevent inclusion of more than 220 people, it was agreed Survivors and their families should be prioritized. River Heights residents were thus involved as serving volunteers, and in other roles, though several also attended the dinner when we realized a few spaces were available.

The words of the Reverend Stan McKay led us into our meal:

It is a great honour to be with you Survivors of the Assiniboia School. It is a great honour to see families together. It is a great honour to see some little children in the room. I think our healing journeys are very much about how we can care for each other, care for ourselves, care for the Earth—so I come tonight with a very simple message. I was asking one of the wise women in the room about how to say "dream" in Anishinaabe. And I think what this will do, this gathering of Survivors and their families and their friends, is to bring back the dream, especially if the stories are funny and life is healing as you come together. So, I came tonight to pay honour to you who all survived this institution down the street. . . . The vision that you carry is needed for our families and our community . . . you must tell the stories, and you must tell the stories, and it's wonderful. . . . I hope that tomorrow you will feel strong in spirit, you will feel strong with stories to share because in a world where people are silent the spirit decreases, and our children have no future. So, dream on my friends. Dream everyday of all the possibilities given to you and

our gift from our Elders, from our ancestors. It's time to
pick up your bundles, and walk the good road.

Theodore Fontaine, a Survivor from the initial group of 1958 students
and a member of the SGC, also spoke and introduced Sister Jean Ell,
the former cook, telling of how she left loaves of bread out for them
to "steal." Father Alarie, a former teacher, was there to represent
school staff. All the while, Daniel Highway, as our emcee, kept the
event lively and fun.

The next day, we were back to the school site, this time in tents
upon the former school fields. Here, the students had played hockey,
football, baseball, and curling. The weather was even more miserable than the previous day, but the pipe ceremony encouraged us to
see the cleansing work performed by the rain. The tents kept us dry,
if not warm.

As the events of the day were underway, we were faced with a
surfeit of remembrances. In addition to the interviews carried out,
the cameras carried by the young people from JustTV, a program for
inner-city youth that provides them audio-visual training, as well as
from the university team, were busy. Conversations about the school
abounded. In many cases, groups of Survivors spontaneously took
the stage to share their memories.

At the time, I was not as fully immersed in these events as I would
have liked. In the moment, I viewed my primary role as that of host,
helping the Survivors and former students feel welcome and looked
after. It was not until reviewing the video and audio files that I was
able to more fully take in what unfolded within the space of the
reunion. The knowledge shared by the Survivors was direct and
sincere.

Knowledge was gathered in a sacred space where the spiritual
source of that knowledge was frequently acknowledged. The relationships that made possible the reunion, and that persist after it, ensured
a degree of relational accountability was established in preparing for
the reunion and to carry us forward together into the future. What

took place was an opening, a gathering, where many separate journeys came together in a spirit of communion. Each brought their individual story into the space of the reunion, aligned it or contrasted it with those of others, and found opportunity for healing, remembrance, laughter, or sorrow.

Sadly, some Survivors were unable to attend. I think of Joe Malcolm, whose family attended the dinner and whose nephews performed the next day. Joe was a member of the SGC and contributed much with his calm and practical insight about how to make such an event possible. Joe died only weeks before the reunion. He came home from a Sunday cruise night, when car aficionados like Joe gather to share their joy in classic automobile restoration. Joe was feeling unwell and passed away in the night.

We remembered and honoured Joe, and all the former Assiniboia students who are gone. Guided by their memory, something powerful took place that day. This book, a gathering of some of the remembrances shared, juxtaposed with items from the Assiniboia archive, reflects that moment. There is no conclusion to be offered here. There is no summary of the key messages. The Survivors' voices, and those of Assiniboia, are complicated and resist being forced into neat and tidy narratives. Indigenous residential schools were spaces of destruction, and also were spaces where young Indigenous people experienced, and sometimes even enjoyed, multiple facets of life.

In assisting the Survivors and former students in pulling together this book and reclaiming their school, I, along with others such as Morgan Sizeland Fontaine, who played a significant role in editing and obtaining images for the volume, have worked to preserve this feeling of gathering. Their voices are at the centre of this gathering, while my contributions to the discussion are placed sporadically in the text so they do not overstep their intended role. You are invited to join us in remembering Assiniboia, through this book which is itself a reunion, and in ensuring that this memory persists in Winnipeg and beyond.

THE LEGACY OF REUNION, REMEMBRANCE, AND RECLAMATION

Theodore Fontaine

A reunion of former students of the Assiniboia Indian Residential School in 2013 was the initial attempt at bringing former students and supporters together. Planning and execution of such a gathering was challenging. Even the Creator expressed the sentiment that this would be a day for cleansing. It rained heavily the whole day. Thanks to the RCMP, we were sheltered with tipis on the playing fields of our former school. One Survivor, strongly reviving his traditions and culture, brought his own tipi with him.

In spite of the soggy day, quite a number of former students came out to enjoy visiting and reminiscing about those bygone days. The majority of Survivors who participated were from the early years of Assiniboia. Sitting together on blankets with hot tea in our hands, we exchanged stories—good, sad, and bad. Friendships were redis-covered and renewed, and laughter floated up with the smoke from our smudge. It seemed that the spirits of many were with us, unseen, yet supporting our remembrances.

The second reunion was held in September 2015. Attended by Survivors and family members, and some River Heights residents and church representatives, we were warmly welcomed on the grounds by the Canadian Centre for Child Protection. The staff set up chairs, microphone, and speakers, provided refreshments, and gave mean-ingful gifts to each Survivor. The RCMP tipi was again erected on the grass, and the Creator brought bright sun and healing winds to our gathering.

The third reunion, held 23 and 24 June 2017, was well attended by Survivors as well as people from the surrounding community of River Heights. The reunion sparked media interest and drew in the leadership of area churches, led by Westworth United. Many area and faith community volunteers contributed their time and talents

to hosting a tea for Survivors and families, a reception and community dinner with entertainment. These events were an overwhelming success, attended by Survivors, their families, and River Heights
past and current community residents. The attendees were treated
to an exceptional evening, an opportunity for building relationships,
for understanding the true meaning of reconciliation, and for putting
words into action.

The reunion included public tours of the former classrooms building, generously hosted by the Canadian Centre for Child Protection,
with information talks given by Survivors and former staff. In huge
tents on the grounds, we shared food and entertainment, interviews
and discussion groups, and restored friendships and made new ones.

Former students and classmates met as Survivors within different groups, finding those who had attended in the same years. They
remembered, laughed, and compared their perceptions and assessments of the evolution of the Indian residential schools they had
attended. They expressed hope and resolve that the realities of
these experiences would not disappear from the history of Canada.
Too much has already been lost.

Figure 70. Theodore Fontaine in former Assiniboia classrooms building, 2017.

Critical to our sense of success was the overwhelming partic
ipation of River Heights community residents, their interest and
questions, their astonishment at learning about this Indian school
that had operated in their midst for so many years, and, most of all,
the empathy they exhibited and the caring they demonstrated.

We Survivors were blessed that day and evening, with expressions
of love and caring, the release of tears and laughter, and the opportunity to give voice to our childhood experiences. We never forget those
many former students who left this realm too early, who couldn't wait
for a reunion, and left us knowing that our love and remembrance of
them is still and always will be a part of our lives.

We were also truly blessed by the participation of Father Laurent
Alarie, former teacher, and Sister Jean Ell, head cook at Assiniboia,
both beloved and appreciated for their kindness and service when
as teenagers we were like lost souls, and today, for their enduring
memories of us as we were and as we are.

Figure 71. Theodore Fontaine with Father Alarie and Sister Ell, September 2019.

We are thankful to the Canadian Centre for Child Protection, the RCMP, Westworth United Minister Loraine MacKenzie Shepherd, planning committee members from area churches, Métis community members Beth and Brian Barton and Boadicea Barton-Bailey, Andrew Woolford and his team from the University of Manitoba, and many others whose contributions to this reunion were immeasurable.

These many community leaders have continued to bring Indigenous and non-Indigenous people together, starting with River Heights and West Winnipeg, and expanding into multifaith dialogues hosted in churches, synagogues, mosques, and temples across this city. These ongoing sharing and discussion groups are meaningful acts of reconciliation, building the strength of cross-cultural understanding and relationships throughout our communities.

Our small group of Assiniboia Survivors have pursued our vision to ensure the legacy of Assiniboia endures. Throughout these years, we have been exceptionally privileged to work in conjunction with Andrew Woolford, University of Manitoba professor of sociology and criminology, and former president of the International Association of Genocide Scholars. Andrew has extensively published research and hosted international study and conference events focused on Indian boarding schools and residential schools operated in the United States and Canada, within the context of genocide, redress, decolonization, and destruction. His multiyear coordination and support to Survivors from the Assiniboia Indian Residential School aims to advance public knowledge, reconciliation, commemoration, and reclamation of this school by its former students.

The Survivors committee has moved forward to incorporate the Assiniboia Indian Residential School Legacy Group, a non-profit organization, with the goals to preserve and commemorate the Assiniboia Indian Residential School site, to secure land there for both a commemorative marker and a meeting space on the playing fields, to publish this book of Assiniboia remembrance, and to raise funds for future initiatives. These goals are among the outcomes of the 2017 reunion.

On 30 September 2018, another major event took place on the Assiniboia playing fields. A huge powwow, led by Wab Kinew and coordinated by Grace Redhead, attracted over 200 participants including Survivors, First Nations, and River Heights community members to celebrate Orange Shirt Day, a public-awareness event held since 2013 to raise awareness of the Indian residential school system. The event was envisioned to bring the community together to celebrate the resilience of Survivors and their families while honouring those that have passed on to the spirit world. Orange Shirt Day has been formally recognized in Manitoba by a legislative initiative led by second-generation Survivor Wab Kinew.

We are committed to ensure that the Assiniboia Indian Residential School at 621 Academy Road is not forgotten in the city of Winnipeg. Following meetings between our board of directors and city officials, a small parcel of land has been approved for placement of a permanent memorial to replace the old marker that occupied the spot in front of the original school's location. City planners and architects have been gracious and very professional in supporting and assisting our Board.

Demolition and privatization of the historic buildings and lands at 615 and 621 Academy Road have resulted in loss of significant historical meaning for our city. The original buildings, dating back to 1915, were lost after providing shelter and classrooms for orphaned and removed children, veterans, and Indian children through many decades until the 1980s. All that remains is our classrooms building, originally the Julia Clark School. This single remaining historic treasure is now designated by the City of Winnipeg as a historical resource, and by destiny is now home to the Canadian Centre for Child Protection.

We are working with all three levels of government to commemorate the grassy playing fields behind the school site, running alongside Wellington Crescent and the railway tracks. This is the land where Indian children found their freedom, revived their Indigenous language skills, and sought comfort and joy from their "family" of other children.

Figure 72. Theodore Fontaine in former Assiniboia classrooms building.

This green space allows a quiet place for reflection and remembrance. It is the only place we have left to seek peace in our residential schools history, to gather with hope and friendship, and to honour those children who were lost to Canada through their residential schools experience.

The Assiniboia Indian Residential School Legacy Group is seeking development of a reconciliation framework to reclaim and save this historic land for future generations of our children and grandchildren, and for all those of River Heights families who join with us in reconciliation. We have strong support from Andrew Woolford, University of Manitoba professor of architecture Herbert Enns, and City of Winnipeg officials.

Our aspiration is to gain heritage designation for the playing fields in their entirety, to have a portion of this land recognized for Indian residential schools ceremonial and meeting purposes, to ensure the Assiniboia site is designated with a commemorative marker, and to protect the heritage of former students and River Heights residents through collaborative acts of reconciliation.

We urge all River Heights and area residents, former and present, to join with us, the City of Winnipeg and the University of Manitoba, to actively support these aspirations of the former students and Survivors of Assiniboia.

Andrew Woolford has written that Indigenous residential schools were spaces of destruction. Many separate journeys came together in 2013, 2015, and 2017 in a spirit of communion. In these acts of reconciliation, we found spaces for healing, remembrance, sorrow, laughter, and friendship.

May we now come together as one community to make space for ceremony and commemoration, space for preservation and reconciliation, space to create this legacy of our shared journey.

May the love and peace of the Creator, and all who have left before us, be reflected in our spirits as the stars in the celestial heavens shine brightly to light our way, to guide and protect us.

Indigenous and non-Indigenous together, may we close our circle to honour this land and its legacy of freedom and hope for children.

Gichi miigwech.

VALEDICTORIAN ADDRESS

The long awaited Graduation day finally dawns after having looked forward to it for twelve years or more. When we first entered Assiniboia, feeling strange and alone, little did we realize that one day we would be leaving it with such a mixed sensation of contentment and sadness we are experiencing at this moment.

Reminiscences over our past school life will always be a source of joy and inspiration for the future. We will always remember the salient highlights of the years we passed here. Occasions such as the past Graduation ceremonies, the M.A.M.I. meetings, the speech contests, the parties and picnics, the annual carnival, the sports activities and others will never be forgotten.

The event which surpassed all others by far was the celebration of the twenty-fifth Anniversary of Priesthood of our dearest Principal, Reverend Father Omer Robidoux O.M.I.. What an opportunity for us to express our sincere appreciation and heartfelt thanks to Father for the tremendous help he so untiringly gives us! Today again, we are extremely happy to assure him of our high esteem.

To our dearest parents we extend our greatest appreciation. For the years they have dedicated to our health, happiness and education, we are truly grateful. Today we are greatly aware of how much they have done for us in the past, the little things, which we selfishly thought were entitled to us. Along with our gratitude we give them our love and assurance for they have proved themselves to be the best parents in the world.

We will not forget either our school teachers and supervisors. They each gave us methods in study and manners, but they gave us far more. They gave us their philosophy of life. While our teachers lit the spark of the learning torch for us, our supervisors helped and encouraged us.

On behalf of my fellow graduates, I should like, at this time to thank the staff for their friendship through the years. We also thank the administrative, maintenance and kitchen personnel for making our stay here a pleasant one.

At this stage of our life, we know that a great responsibility awaits us for our people need us and depend on us. Let us give them the best we have in return for all that we have received. And so we bid farewell to the Assiniboia School. We wish her, her teachers and the students who pass through each year, the best of fortune and continued success. As for us, we will soon separate and go to different parts of the province and beyond, but the bond which will unite us is and will be our dear Alma Mater, Assiniboia Residential High School.

Audrey McPherson

Figure 73. Audrey McPherson's valedictorian address from the 1964–65 Assiniboia yearbook.

ACKNOWLEDGEMENTS

This book, and our broader efforts to ensure the commemoration of Assiniboia, have been made possible by so many people. Our sincere apologies if we have forgotten to include anyone.

Miigwech to the Survivors and intergenerational Survivors who have assisted in planning and carrying out our activities. Listed alphabetically, they are: Dorothy Ann Crate, Theodore (Ted) Fontaine, Daniel Highway, Mabel Horton, Toni Kipling, Joe Malcolm, Rudy Okimaw, Caroline Perreault, Betty Ross, David Rundle, and Rosa Walker. We also acknowledge the work of Herbert Enns, Rhonda Forgues, Jessica Paley, Murray Peterson, Aron Skworchinski, Ruth Wiwchar, and Andrew Woolford.

This book grew out of the Assiniboia reunions that were held in 2015 and 2017. These events were made possible by the efforts of many people in our community. We would like to thank Sandy Addison, Father Laurent Alerie, Chris Barnes, Beth and Brian Barton, Boadicea Barton-Bailey, The Beaulieu Boys, Alyssa Bird, Bernard Boland, Mayor Brian Bowman, Shira Brand, Clark Brownie, Christopher Calesso, Debbie Cielen, Raymond Currie, Erica Daniels, Daly de Gagne, Noelle Dietrich, Sister Jean Ell, Helen Fallding, Stephanie Fehr, Martina Fisher, Arlene Flatfoot, Carmella Fontaine, Morgan Sizeland Fontaine, James Gacek, Emily Gerbrandt, Irene Greenwood, Nancy Hodgson, Paul James, Joan Jarvis, Belle Jarniewski, Annamaria Johnson, Laura Johnson, Wanda June, Peter Karari, Tracey Kennedy, Leslie Kenny, Kathy Knowles, Dave Labdon, Tricia Logan, Matthew Loxley, Karen Lumley, Katelyn Mackenzie, Loraine MacKenzie Shepherd, Jackie Markstrom, Stan McKay, Scott McMurchy, Catherine Mitchell, Ry Moran, Paul Murphy, John Orlikow, Rebecca Parkinson, Kevin Palendat, Dale Plewak, Stephanie Pyne, Gary Robson, Rachelle Rocque, Chris Rutkowski, Georgina Sabesky, Susan Scott, Sarah Story, Chris Trott, Randy Turner, Tannis Webster, Elnora Wiebe, Joan Wilton, Dorcas Windsor, Avery Wolaniuk, and Prairie Skye Young Brown.

Many foundations, organizations, groups, and individuals have contributed to our efforts: Assiniboine Credit Union, the Archdiocese of St. Boniface, the Archdiocese of Winnipeg, Broadway Florists, the Canadian Centre for Child Protection, Chocolatier Constance Popp, Congregation Shaarey Zedek, Cornelia Bean, the Diocese of Rupert's Land, Fisher River Cree Nation, Harvest Bakery, High Tea Bakery, JustTV, Darren Lavallee, the Manitoba Multifaith Council, the National Centre for Truth and Reconciliation, Neechi Foods, the Office of City Councillor John Orlikow, River Heights/Fort Garry Ward, Peace Hills Trust, the RCMP, Red River College Culinary Arts Program, royalties from *This Benevolent Experiment: Indigenous Boarding Schools, Genocide, and Redress in Canada and the United States* (University of Manitoba Press and University of Nebraska Press), St. Aidan's Anglican Church, St. Andrew's River Heights United Church, St. John's College (University of Manitoba), St. John XXIII Roman Catholic Church, St. Kateri Tekakwitha Aboriginal Catholic Church, the United Church of Canada Justice and Reconciliation Fund, the United Way Building Blocks Program, Voila Design Studio, Westworth United Church, the *Winnipeg Free Press*, and the Winnipeg Foundation.

Images and other historical materials were located with the support of several archives and archivists: Archives Deschâtelets-NDC (Elizabeth Darsigny), Archives of Manitoba (Tracey Goncalves), Centre Du Patrimoine (Giles Lesage and Julie Reid), Library and Archives Canada (Joel Cyr and Stéphanie Hurtubise), National Centre for Truth and Reconciliation (Anne Lindsay and Karen Ashbury), Shingwauk Residential School Centre (Krista McCracken), University of Manitoba Archives and Special Collections (Nicole Courrier and James Kominowski), Western Development Museum (Elizabeth A. Scott), Whitemouth Photography (George Penner), and the *Winnipeg Free Press* (Stacy Thidrickson and Mike Aporius).

We are pleased to acknowledge the generous financial support of the Social Sciences and Humanities Research Council of Canada through the Manitoba Research Alliance grant: Partnering for Change – Community-based Solutions for Aboriginal and Inner-City Poverty.

216

John Loxley, Elizabeth Comack, Lynne Fernandez, and Jess Klassen have provided wonderful collegial support for this project and we appreciate their patience in its early, developmental stages.

Our thanks to the University of Manitoba Press, including David Carr, Jill McConkey, David Larsen, Ariel Gordon, Barbara Romanik, and Glenn Bergen, for their continued support and the time and care put into helping us produce this volume.

APPENDIX:
ASSINIBOIA INDIAN RESIDENTIAL SCHOOL TIMELINE

1600s

As early as 1620, French missionary boarding schools were opened for Indian youth. However, it was not until the nineteenth century that the official assimilation policies and federal system of residential schooling for Indigenous children was established.

1700s

Throughout the 1700s the British imperial government began its efforts of settlement and nation building which required clearing the lands of Indigenous peoples.

- **The Royal Proclamation of 1763:** The Proclamation provides the framework for imperial expansion from coast to coast and establishes the treaty-making process and reservation system to acquire said Indigenous lands.

1800s

Throughout the 1800s, the imperial government intensified its settlement and expansion efforts. During this time, the assimilation of Indigenous peoples was recognized as a means to this end. Early Indian residential schools were built and run by Protestant, Catholic, Anglican, and Methodist churches and were supported by the federal government because they were seen as an effective way to put an end to increasing Indigenous resistance. By the end of the century, there were forty-five Indian residential and industrial schools across Canada.

- **The Gradual Civilization Act of 1857:** The Civilization act lays the groundwork for a legal policy for the assimilation of Indigenous peoples.

- **Canadian Confederation, 1867:** Confederation legally establishes the Dominion of Canada, which originally includes Nova Scotia, New Brunswick, Ontario, and Quebec, but would later include the additional six provinces and three territories that make up what we now call Canada.

- **The Dominion Lands Act of 1872:** The Act offers incentive for those wishing to settle in what would later be the prairie provinces.

- **The Indian Act of 1876:** This first draft, and its later amendments, generates laws that only apply to Indigenous peoples, lands, and cultural practices.

- **The Davin Report of 1879:** Following the establishment of the Indian Affairs Department and the Indian Act, member of Parliament Nicholas Flood Davin files a report that recommends an assimilation strategy through the use of boarding schools modelled after those already established in the United States.

- **1885:** The Northwest Rebellion, under the leadership of Louis Riel, demands status and land recognition for Métis peoples.

1900s

During the early 1900s the federal government entered into an official agreement with churches in support of the residential schooling system. By the 1930s, there were eighty schools across Canada, and it is estimated that 150,000 Indigenous children passed through its system. Mid-century, critiques of poor living conditions and underfunding prompted calls for the schools' closures, and by 1960 the number of schools reduced from eighty to sixty; by 1979 that number was reduced to twelve. While measures were put in place to begin the integration of Indigenous children into the public schooling system, the residential schooling system persisted into the late-twentieth century. Assiniboia Indian Residential School operated during this time. By the end of the century, Survivors began speaking out on the impact of the residential schools, prompting the Royal Commission on Aboriginal Peoples and its final report that recommended an inquiry into the impact of school system.

- **1920**: Residential school attendance becomes compulsory for children between the ages of seven and fifteen.

- **1922**: Chief Medical Officer for Indian Affairs, Dr. Peter Henderson Bryce, publishes a report titled, *The Story of a National Crime: Being a Record of the Health Conditions of the Indians of Canada from 1904 to 1921.* The report documented Dr. Bryce's 1907 assessment of the health conditions at numerous residential schools and children's deaths related to poor construction, sanitation, ventilation, diet, and a lack of medical care.

- **1940**: Provincial curriculum standards are applied to residential schools.

- **1950s**: The federal government initiates a new strategy of First Nations children's integration into public schooling.

- **1951**: The Indian Act undergoes major revisions that reflect the government's intention to further integrate Indigenous peoples into Canadian society.

- **1958**: On 2 September 1958 Assiniboia Indian Residential School opens as the first residential high school in the province of Manitoba. At this time, it is run by the Oblates of Mary Immaculate.

- **1959**: A grade eleven class is added to the Assiniboia school.

- **1960**: A grade twelve class is added to the Assiniboia school.

- **1961**: Assiniboia graduates its first class.

  The 1961 special joint committee of the Senate and the House of Commons recommends closing residential schools.

- **1962**: Grade eight is discontinued at the Assiniboia school.

- **1963**: The Glassco Commission recommends the closing of residential schools and the integration of Indigenous students into the public school system.

- **1965**: An inspection of Assiniboia reveals inadequate, overcrowded, and poorly ventilated and "inadequate" living conditions.

  Grade nine is discontinued at the Assiniboia school.

- **1967**:

  Assiniboia is converted into a hostel that houses Indigenous students who are integrated into Winnipeg public schools. The fifth Pan-American Games are held in Winnipeg.

- **1969**: The Canadian Federal Government takes over the operation of residential schools including Assiniboia residential high school.

- **1973**: Assiniboia closes on 30 June 1973.

- **1982**: The Constitution Act is amended to include the rights of Indigenous, Inuit, and Métis peoples.

- **1984**: The main building of Assiniboia Indian Residential School is demolished to make way for an RCMP forensic laboratory.

- **1996**: The last residential school closes, and the final report of the Royal Commission on Aboriginal Peoples calls for an inquiry into the impact of the Indian Residential School system.

- **1998**: The Aboriginal Healing Foundation is established by the federal government, meant to distribute $350 million in reparations over the next ten years.

2000s

At the turn of the century, the impact of the residential school system on Indigenous lives, communities, and cultures was increasingly coming to light. During this time, class-action lawsuits were announced. This action spurred multiple reparation attempts by the federal government and ultimately led to the establishment of the Truth and Reconciliation Commission of Canada.

- **2005**: National Chief of the Assembly of First Nations, Phil Fontaine, announces a class-action lawsuit against the Canadian government.

- **2006**: The Indian Residential Schools Settlement Agreement (IRSSA) is signed by representatives of some Survivors, the churches, the Assembly of First Nations, and the federal government.

- **2008**: The federal government issues an official public apology for the harms of the residential school system, delivered by Prime Minister Stephen Harper in the House of Commons.

  The Truth and Reconciliation Commission of Canada is tasked with documenting the harms of the residential school system and providing recommendations for reconciliation.

- **2015**: The Truth and Reconciliation Commission of Canada offices are closed and the work is transferred to the National Centre for Truth and Reconciliation.

NOTES

PART I: THE RESIDENTIAL YEARS, 1958–67

1. We include the student's home community as listed in the Assiniboia Residential School records. Where the community now identifies itself by its Indigenous name, we provide that name with the former name in brackets.

2. Later known as the Rehabilitation Centre for Children.

3. Sihko is Jane Glennon's nickname. It is a Cree word meaning "Weasel," and her siblings tell her she received it because of her dark hair and lighter complexion (see https://mediaindigena.com/sihkos-story-residential-school-remembrances-of-a-little-brown-white-girl/). Originally published as J. Glennon, *Sihkos' Story, Part IV: Assiniboia Residential School*, n.d., https://mediaindigena.com/sihkos-story-part-iv-assiniboia-residential-school/. Our thanks to Rick Harp and Media Indigena for permission to republish.

4. Transcribed oral interviews were only lightly edited for grammar and flow. All interviews took place between June and August 2017.

5. See the Truth and Reconciliation Commission of Canada, *A Knock on the Door: The Essential History of Residential Schools* (Winnipeg: University of Manitoba Press, 2015).

6. He is referring to the St. Joseph's Indian Residential School in Fort William, Ontario.

7. St. Margaret's Indian Residential School, which was also known as the Fort Frances Indian Residential School.

8. In 1970, Port Arthur, Fort William, Neebing, and McIntyre amalgamated to form the city of Thunder Bay.

9. Including the McIntosh Indian Residential School.

10. See Erica Daniels, *Run as One: The Journey of the Front Runners*, CBCShortDocs, https://www.cbc.ca/shortdocs/shorts/run-as-one-the-journey-of-the-front-runners .

11. The 2017 North American Indigenous Games were held in Toronto from 17 to 21 July. See: http://naig2017.to/.

PART II: THE HOSTEL YEARS, 1967–73

1. Fort Alexander Indian Residential School.

2. Ms. Fisher is referring to the "pass system," which was instituted by the Canadian government in 1885 to restrict Indigenous movement in Canada. See, for example, *Report of the Royal Commission on Aboriginal Peoples* (Ottawa: Royal Commission on Aboriginal Peoples, 1996). See also, Alex Williams's 2016 documentary *The Pass System: Life Under Segregation in Canada*, http://thepasssystem.ca/.

PART III: ASSINIBOIA AND THE ARCHIVE

1. Government of Canada, *Assiniboia Indian Residential School IAP School Narrative* (Ottawa: Government of Canada, 2012), 1.

2. Ibid., 1; Indian Record, "Gov't Takes Over Residences," *Indian Record* 32, nos. 8 and 9 (August–September 1969): 4.

3. E.G. Fulson, Letter to Howard D Green, RG 10, Vol. 10394, File 506/25-13, Library and Archives Canada, Ottawa, 1958.

4. "The Essentials of a Catholic School," *Indian Record* 20, no. 9 (November 1957): 2; B. Guimont, "Manitoba Catholic Indians Plead for Denominational Education," *Indian Record* 20, no. 9 (November 1957): 6.

5. "The Essentials of a Catholic School," 2.

6. D. Ragan, Letter to Indian Affairs Branch, Department of Citizenship and Immigration, RG 10, Vol. 10394, File 506/25-13, Library and Archives Canada, Ottawa, 1958; L. Brown, Memorandum to the Deputy Minister Re: Veterans' Home – Winnipeg, 19 March 1958, RG 10, Vol. 10394, File 506/25-13, Library and Archives Canada, Ottawa.

7. D. Ragan, Letter to R.F. Davey, Superintendent of Education, on finding a name for the new school in the former Veterans' Home, 30 April 1958, RG 10, Vol. 10394, File 506/25-13, Library and Archives Canada, Ottawa. Academy Road is named after St. Mary's Academy, a private girls' school located at the start of the road.

8. R.F. Davey, Letter to Regional Supervisor, Manitoba, Superintendent of Education, 6 May 1958, RG 10, Vol. 10394, File 506/25-13, Library and Archives Canada, Ottawa.

9. R.F. Davey, Letter to Regional Supervisor, Manitoba, Superintendent of Education, 9 May 1958, RG 10, Vol 10394, File 506/25-13, Library and Archives Canada, Ottawa.

10. "Assiniboia Residential School Opens in Winnipeg," *Indian Record* 21, no. 6 (June 1958).

11. D. Ragan, Letter to R.F. Davey, Superintendent of Education, 30 April 1958, RG 10, Vol 10394, File 506/25-13, Library and Archives Canada, Ottawa; see also R.F. Davey, Letter to Regional Supervisor, 6 May 1958.

12. As the grandchild of a Barnardo's home child "orphan," whose great-grandmother was deemed unfit based on her poverty, I am inclined to see "orphan" as a loaded and ideological label rather than an objective condition.

13. "To Erect $65,000 Children's Home," *Winnipeg Tribune*, 31 May 1915; "Will Build New Children's Home: $90,000 to Be Spent This Season – Await $25000 Government Grant," *Winnipeg Evening Tribune*, 5 June 1915.

14. Lillian Gibbons, "This Home Has 160 Beds to Be Made Every Day," *Winnipeg Tribune*, 29 September 1939, 9.

15. "Children's Home Makes Progress: Annual Meeting Hears Good Reports from All Departments," *Winnipeg Evening Tribune*, 26 October 1923, 6; "Board of Children's Home Reports Much Good Work Done Throughout Last Year," *Winnipeg Tribune*, 17 October 1940, 9.

16. "Children's Home Sold as Veterans' Hospital," *Winnipeg Tribune*, 5 January 1945.

17. Ibid.; "Children's Home Buys Fowler Residence," *Winnipeg Tribune*, 13 April 1945; "Mrs. W.H. Collum President of Children's Home Board," *Winnipeg Tribune*, 17 October 1947, 7. It is not clear, based on the evidence reviewed, whether or not any of the residents of the Children's Home were Indigenous.

18. Government of Canada, *Assiniboia Indian Residential School IAP School Narrative*.

19. D. Ragan, Letter to Superintendent of Education R.F. Davey, 8 July 1958, RG 10, Vol. 10394, File 506/25-13, Library and Archives Canada, Ottawa; Winnipeg Regional Office, Letter to Indian Affairs Branch, Ottawa, 25 July 1958, RG 10, Vol. 10394, File 506/25-13, Library and Archives Canada, Ottawa.

20. Truth and Reconciliation Commission of Canada, *Final Report of the Truth and Reconciliation Commission of Canada, Canada's Residential Schools: The History, Part II* (Ottawa: Truth and Reconciliation Commission of Canada, 2015), 183.

21. Rev. I. Tourigny, OMI, Provincial Superior, Missionaires Oblats de Marie Immaculée, Letter to Colonel Jones, Director, Indian Affairs, 29 May 1958, RG 10, Vol. 10394, File 506/25-13, Library and Archives Canada, Ottawa; R.F. Davey, Superintendent of Education, Letter to Rev. I Tourigny, OMI, Provincial Superior, Mission-

aires Oblats de Marie Immaculée, 10 June 1958, RG 10, Vol. 10394, File 506/25-13, Library and Archives Canada, Ottawa.

22. "Assiniboia Residential School Opens in Winnipeg," *Indian Record* 21, no. 6 (June 1958).

23. Ibid.

24. Ibid.

25. Government of Canada, *Assiniboia Indian Residential School IAP School Narrative.*

26. D. Ragan Letter to Indian Affairs Re: Admissions to Assiniboia School for Hostel Accommodation, 3 August 1958, RG 10, Vol. 6860, File 506/25-2-018, Library and Archives Canada, Ottawa; D. Ragan, Letter to Indian Affairs Branch, Department of Citizenship and Immigration, RG 10, Vol. 6860, File 506/25-2-018, 5 Aug 1958, Library and Archives Canada, Ottawa.

27. Government of Canada, *Assiniboia Indian Residential School IAP School Narrative.*

28. "Assiniboia High School Graduates First Students," Indian Record 24, no. 6 (June 1961): 1.

29. R.F. Davey, Letter to the Regional Supervisor of Indian Agencies, 18 August 1958, RG 10, Vol. 6860, File 506/25-2-018, Library and Archives Canada, Ottawa.

30. For more on the Indian Act and its amendments, see J.R. Miller, *Skyscrapers Hide the Heavens: A History of Indian-White Relations in Canada* (Toronto: University of Toronto Press, 1989); John S. Milloy, *A Historical Overview of Indian-Government Relations 1755–1940* (Ottawa: Department of Indian Affairs and Northern Development, 1992); John S. Milloy, "The Early Indian Acts: Developmental Strategy and Constitutional Change," in *Sweet Promises: A Reader on Indian-White Relations in Canada*, ed. J.R. Miller, 145–154 (Toronto: University of Toronto Press, 1991).

31. See Theodore Fontaine, *Broken Circle: The Dark Legacy of Canada's Residential School System, A Memoir* (Victoria: Heritage Press, 2010); Andrew Woolford, *This Benevolent Experiment: Indigenous Boarding Schools, Genocide and Repair in Canada and the United States* (Winnipeg and Lincoln: University of Manitoba Press and University of Nebraska Press, 2015).

32. See, for example, a 1958 application for admission for a student from Fisher River, where it is noted, "The parents of this girl feel they will lose control of her if she stays on this reserve. She is very interested in her school work and it is felt she would do much better at residential school." For another student from God's Lake it is stated, "Pupil caused considerable trouble at Fort Alexander School last term." RG 10, Vol. 6860, File 506/25-2-018, Library and Archives Canada, Ottawa.

33. Group discussion with Assiniboia Indian Residential School Survivors, 28 July 2016.

34. Sath Square, "Reaching Out to New Horizons: Indian Youth New to City Life Review their Impressions, Adjustments," *Leisure Magazine, Winnipeg Free Press*, 28 December 1968, 7.

35. Jane Glennon in this volume, see pp. 33-38

36. Omer Robidoux, Letter to Mr. and Mrs. William George Guimond, 14 Sept 1958, RG 10, Vol. 6860, File 506/25-2-018 Library and Archives Canada, Ottawa.

37. Jane Glennon in this volume, see pp. 33-38; Obituary for Elizabeth Victoria Hart (née Menow), *Winnipeg Free Press*, 10 November 2001: "Mom said it was difficult to be away from her family but that she learned to enjoy school"; Truth and Reconciliation Commission of Canada, *Final Report: The History, Part II*, 365.

38. Group discussion with Assiniboia Indian Residential School Survivors, 28 July 2016. See also Theodore Fontaine's chapter, pp. 16-33.

39. "Grade IX Report" *Assiniboia News* (1958–59): 8.

40. "The Essentials of a Catholic School," *Indian Record* 20, no. 9 (November 1957): 2.

41. The Assiniboia newsletter, titled *Assiniboia News* and *Assiniboia Highlights*, is worthy of a study on its own. At the two reunions hosted to date, Survivors enjoyed spending time with these documents and revisiting the memories captured in their pages. Nine volumes of the newsletter were produced between 1958 and 1967, with as many as three issues included in each volume. The editorship and reporting for the newsletter rested with members of the student body, under the oversight of a teacher "advisor." It is not clear how active or heavy an editorial hand the "advisors" took in producing the newsletters. According to the newsletter's first editor, Julie Morriseau, the main purpose of the newsletter was "to inform our parents about academic, arts, social, and sports events and other school activities." "From the Editor's Pen," *Assiniboia News* (1958–59): 8.

42. "Grade IX Report," *Assiniboia News* (1958–59): 8.

43. "Special Report," *Assiniboia Highlights* 5, no. 3 (1964): 2.

44. Theda Bradshaw, "Winter Carnival at Assiniboia School," *Indian Record* 25, no. 2 (March–April 1962): 7.

45. "General News," *Assiniboia Highlights* 5, no. 1 (1963): 7

46. Theda Bradshaw, "Winter Carnival at Assiniboia School," 7.

47. J.D. Kinnie, Superintendent Clandeboye Indian Agency, Letter to D. Ragan, Regional Supervisor of Indian Agencies, Winnipeg, 5 November 1968, Manitoba Regional Office - Audit Reports, Assiniboia Students' residence, Manitoba Region, 1959-1969, File 501/16-2-018, RG 10, Box 232, 32, Library and Archives Canada, Ottawa.

48. Rev. I. Tourigny, Letter Colonel Laval Fortier, Deputy Minister of Citizenship, Requesting East Wing Addition, December 1958, RG 10,

Vol. 10394, File 506/25-13, Library and Archives Canada, Ottawa; N.M. Jones, Letter to Reverand Liske Re: Request for a Gymnasium and Chapel, 15 August 1961, RG 10, Vol. 10394, File 506/25-13, Library and Archives Canada, Ottawa.

49. "Assiniboia School Athletes," *Indian Record* 22, no. 2 (February 1959).

50. "Assiniboia Pucksters Retain Manitoba Championship," Indian Record 25, no. 3 (May–June 1961): 4.

51. "Chapel, gym set for Indian School," Winnipeg Tribune, 7 April 1965, 27; "Chapel Gymnasium and Five New Graduates for Assiniboia Residential High School," *Indian Record* 29, no. 9 (November 1966): 8.

52. Prairie Provinces Engineer, Letter to the Regional Supervisor, Manitoba, 4 May 1962, RG 10, Vol. 10394, File 506/25-13, Library and Archives Canada, Ottawa.

53. Group discussion with Assiniboia Indian Residential School Survivors, 28 July 2016.

54. D. Davidson, Letter to The Secretary of the Treasury Board, 15 September 1960, RG 10, File 501/16-2-018, Box 232, 32, Library and Archives Canada, Ottawa; R.F. Davey, Letter to O. Robidoux, RG 10, File 501/16-2-018, Box 232, 32, Library and Archives Canada, Ottawa.

55. Group discussion with Assiniboia Indian Residential School Survivors, 28 July 2016.

56. Omer Robidoux, Foreword, *Assiniboia Highlights* 3, no. 2 (1960): 1.

57. Ibid, 2.

58. Ibid, 13.

59. Theda Bradshaw, "Winter Carnival at Assiniboia School," *Indian Record* 25, no. 2 (March–April 1962): 7.

60. On the notion of discipline, see, in general, Michel Foucault, *Discipline and Punish: The Birth of the Prison* (New York: Vintage, 1977.)

61. Omer Robidoux, "From the Principal's Pen," *Assiniboia Highlights* 5, no. 3 (1964): 3.

62. The 5 October 1962 Dietician Report is included in R.F. Davey, Letter to Father Robidoux, 31 October 1962, RG 10, Vol. 10394, File 506/25-13, Library and Archives Canada, Ottawa.

63. Truth and Reconciliation Commission of Canada, *Final Report: The History, Part II*, 295.

64. R.F. Davey, Letter to the Chief of the Education Division, 12 September 1960, RG 10, File 501/16-2-018, Box 232, 32, Library and Archives Canada, Ottawa; R.F. Davey, Memorandum to the Chief of the Education Division, 5 August 1960, RG 10, File 501/16-2-018, Box 232, 32, Library and Archives Canada, Ottawa.

65. G.J. Champagne, Purchasing Manager, La Procure Generale Des Institutions Inc., Letter to N.B. Chappelle, Indian Affairs, 7 February 1968, RG 10, File 501/16-2-018, Box 232, 32, Library and Archives Canada, Ottawa; G.J. Champagne, Letter to R.F. Davey, 15 February 1968, RG 10, File 501/16-2-018, Box 232, 32, Library and Archives Canada, Ottawa.

66. N.B. Chapple, Memo to Director, Education Services, 1 February 1968, RG 10, File 501/16-2-018, Box 232, 32, Library and Archives Canada, Ottawa.

67. See Harold Cardinal, *The Unjust Society* (Vancouver: Douglas and McIntyre, 1999).

68. Harry Hawthorn, ed., *A Survey of the Contemporary Indians of Canada: Economic, Political, Educational Needs and Policies*, 2 vols. (Ottawa: Queen's Printer Press, 1966–1967), http://www.ainc-inac. gc.ca/ai/arp/ls/phi-eng.asp.

69. J.R. Walker, "Glassco Commission Recommends Closing All Indian Schools," *Indian Record* 26, no. 1 (January–February, 1963): 1.

70. The *Indian Record* was a national newspaper founded in 1938 by the Oblates of Mary Immaculate. Issues were published approximately ten times a year from the late 1930s to the mid-1980s. According to a 1957 edition of the paper, it was distributed to "all Catholic mission centers from Coast to Coast, and even beyond the Arctic Circle; high ranking Church and Government official, Members of the Senate and the House of Commons, administration officials of the Indian Affairs Branch and of the Northern Territorial Branch, Indian school teachers across the country and many other prominent citizens." *Indian Record* 20, no. 1 (January, 1957): 1.

71. Editorial, "All Indians in Public School?" *Indian Record* 26, no. 1 (January–February, 1963): 2.

72. Clive Linklater, "Integration or Inter-Sociation," *Indian Record* 26, no. 3 (May–June, 1963).

73. G.W. Isbister, Letter to Reverend Lizée, OMI, Provincial Superior, 2 June 1965, RG 10, Vol. 10394, File 506/25-13, Library and Archives Canada, Ottawa.

74. "Assiniboia School Becomes a Residence," *Indian Record* 30, no. 9 (November 1967): 4.

75. Ibid.

76. Government of Canada, *Assiniboia Indian Residential School IAP School Narrative*.

77. List of articles of clothing supplied to Lucy Nepinak and Doreen McKay, 18 October 1967, Manitoba Regional Office – Audit Reports, Assiniboia Students' residence, Manitoba Region, 1959–1969, File 501/16-2-018, RG 10, Box 232, 32, Library and Archives Canada, Ottawa.

78. Truth and Reconciliation Commission of Canada, *The Survivors Speak* (Ottawa: Truth and Reconciliation Commission of Canada, 2015), 131.

79. Barb Nahwegahbow Birchbark, "Film of '67 Pan Am Games Snub Launches Discussion," *Windspeaker* 33, no. 1 (2015), http://www.ammsa.com/publications/windspeaker/film-%E2%80%9967-pan-am-games-snub-launches-discussion.

80. Truth and Reconciliation Commission of Canada, *The Survivors Speak*, 192.

81. Theda Bradshaw, "What Young Indians are Thinking About," *Winnipeg Free Press*, 26 May 1962, 22.

82. "Meet the Indian," *Assiniboia Highlights* 9, no. 2 (1967): 24–26. "An Indian Centennial Project," *Winnipeg Free Press*, 6 May 1967, 10.

83. "Meet the Indian," 25.

84. "General News," *Assiniboia Highlights* 5, no. 1 (October 1963): 7.

85. "Training Leaders Will Save the Indian Race: Oblate Commission Plans Indian High Schools – Will Encourage Indians to Return to Reserves," *Indian Record* 15, no. 9 (November 1952): 1.

86. "Chapel Gymnasium and Five New Graduates for Assiniboia Residential High School," *Indian Record* 29, no. 9 (November 1966): 8.

87. Agnes Nanowin, "MAMI," *Assiniboia Highlights* 5, no. 3 (1964): 13–14.

88. Truth and Reconciliation Commission of Canada, *The Survivors Speak*, 162.

89. "Assiniboia, Guy Residences Closed," *Indian Record* 36, nos. 6–7 (July-Aug 1973): 11.

90. "Historic Building Doomed," *Winnipeg Free Press*, 23 March 1984, 3; "New RCMP Forensic Lab Announced: $5.3-Million Construction

Starts Monday," *Winnipeg Free Press*, 16 February 1986, 3.

91. For further discussion, see Woolford, *This Benevolent Experiment*.

92. "Training Leaders Will Save the Indian Race: Oblate Commission Plans Indian High Schools – Will Encourage Indians to Return to Reserves," *Indian Record* 15, no. 9 (November 1952): 1.

PART VI: THE CITY OF WINNIPEG REMEMBERS

1. Ry Moran is former director of the National Centre for Truth and Reconciliation.

PART VII: REUNION, REMEMBRANCE, AND RECLAMATION

1. Linda Tuhiwai Smith, *Decolonizing Methodologies: Research and Indigenous Peoples*, 2nd ed. (London: Zed Books, 2012).

2. Embodying Empathy was funded by a Social Sciences and Humanities Research Council Partnership Development Grant. The virtual Indian Residential School, constructed based on the expertise of several residential school Survivors, has been exhibited in several Winnipeg high schools.

3. Some of the group prefer to be referred to as former students rather than Survivors.

4. Shawn Wilson, *Research is Ceremony: Indigenous Research Methods* (Black Point, NS: Fernwood Publishing, 2008).

5. See, for example, Lester-Irabinna Rigney, "Internationalization of an Indigenous Anticolonial Cultural Critique of Research Methodologies: A Guide to Indigenist Research Methodology and Its Principles," *Wicazo Sa Review* 14, no. 2 (1999): 109–21.

6. For Example, see Glen Coulthard's discussion of the "grounded normativity" of Indigenous land-based practices, which

inform decolonizing methodologies. Glen Sean Coulthard, *Red Skins, White Masks: Rejecting the Colonial Politics of Recognition* (Minneapolis: University of Minnesota Press, 2014).

7. Paulette Regan, *Unsettling the Settler Within: Indian Residential Schools, Truth Telling, and Reconciliation in Canada* (Vancouver: University of British Columbia Press, 2011).

8. Woolford, *This Benevolent Experiment.*

9. Eve Tuck, "Suspending Damage: A Letter to Communities," *Harvard Educational Review* 79, no. 3 (2009): 409–27.

10. In particular, Wolfgang Sofsky's sociology of the concentration camp system was an eye-opener in its detailed exploration of the organization of power within this carceral network. Wolfgang Sofsky, *The Order of Terror: The Concentration Camp* (Princeton, NJ: Princeton University Press, 1996).

11. See Brian Schnarch, "Ownership, Control, Access, and Possession (OCAP) or Self-Determination Applied to Research: A Critical Analysis of Contemporary First Nations Research and Some Options for First Nations Communities," *International Journal of Indigenous Health* 1, no. 1 (2004): 80–95.

12. Leanne Betasmoke Simpson, *Dancing on Our Turtle's Back: Stories of Nishnaabeg Re-creation, Resurgence, and a New Emergence* (Winnipeg: Arbeiter Ring, 2011).

13. Leroy Little Bear, "Naturalizing Indigenous Knowledge, Synthesis Paper," University of Saskatchewan, Aboriginal Education Research Centre (2009): 1–28.

14. In March 2017, Canadian Senator Lynn Beyak proclaimed before Senate, "I speak partly for the record, but mostly in memory of the kindly and well-intentioned men and women and their descendants—perhaps some of us here in this chamber—whose remarkable works, good deeds and historical tales in the residential

schools go unacknowledged for the most part and are overshadowed by negative reports." See Kyle Kirkup, "Lynn Beyak Removed from Senate Committee over Residential School Comments." *The Globe and Mail*, 5 April 2017, http://www.theglobeandmail.com/news/politics/beyak-removed-from-senate-committee-over-residential-school-comments/article34610016/.

CONTRIBUTORS

Dorothy Ann Crate (née James) nitisinikason. She was born at God's Lake, Manitoba, on 20 March 1941. She is a fluent Swampy Cree speaker and a residential school Survivor. She has lived in Fisher River Cree Nation for forty-three years, is a mother of four children, and grandmother to seven grandchildren. She is a certified full-time Cree language instructor at Charles Sinclair School in Fisher River and assisted in the development of the Ochékwi Sípí Cree Dictionary. Ékosani, Kinanaskomitinawaw ∇ᑯᐦᓂ ᐸ ᐊ ᑎᒋᓇᐊᐧ.ᐅ.

Since the age of eighteen, **Sister Jean Ell** has devoted herself to a life of service with the Grey Nuns. A psychiatric social worker, she achieved transformative leadership in mental health services for children and young adults. She served in many agencies and charitable organizations, including Children's Aid and the Psychiatry Department of St. Boniface Hospital. In 1977 she established Sara Riel Inc. to provide community-based services, and in 2000, the Jubilee Fund, a registered Canadian charity providing financial access for community non-profits and social enterprises. Now retired, she continues to provide counselling and wellness services to clients.

Martina Fisher, Oshawashko Kiishik Mikisi Ekwe (Blue Sky Eagle Woman), was born and raised in Bloodvein, Manitoba. She is a mother, grandmother, and great-grandmother. She quit school at eighteen years old and returned to school/training in 1987 with the New Careers program and the BSW degree program from 1997 to 2001, when she graduated. She has a social work degree and enjoys working with people; her greatest satisfaction in her work is witnessing the healing journey of Survivors.

Theodore Fontaine is a member and former chief of the Sagkeeng Anicinabe First Nation in Manitoba. He attended the Fort Alexander and Assiniboia Indian Residential Schools from 1948 to 1960. As a youth, he played senior hockey across western Canada before moving north to direct a mineral exploration crew in the Northwest Territories, a formative experience that set him on a lifelong path toward self-discovery and healing. Theodore graduated in civil engineering from Northern Alberta Institute of Technology in 1973 and went on to work extensively in the corporate government and First Nations sectors, including eleven years with the Assembly of Manitoba Chiefs as executive director, lead on Indian Residential Schools, and negotiator of national employment equity claims. Theodore is a regular speaker and media commentator on Indian residential schools and has presented Canadian national bestseller *Broken Circle: The Dark Legacy of Indian Residential Schools, A Memoir* to more than 1,000 audiences in Canada and the United States.

Morgan Sizeland Fontaine is a consulting writer and editor to business, non-profit, and educational initiatives. A graduate of Communications and Public Administration at the University of Manitoba and Red River College, she directed public communications and media relations services to federal, First Nations, health, and social service organizations through a thirty-eight-year professional career. Morgan is a key support in her husband's public education work around Indian residential schools and reconciliation. She also loves animals and nature, and exploring ways for words to illuminate concepts and issues.

Jane Glennon (Woodland Cree), BA, BSW, MSW, is a retired social worker, counsellor, and teacher who currently lives in Prince Albert, Saskatchewan. A member of the Peter Ballantyne Cree Nation, her published work includes "Traditional Parenting," a chapter in the book, *As We See . . . Aboriginal Pedagogy* (University of Saskatchewan Extension Press, 1998).

Hubert (Gilbert) Hart is from Kinosawi Sipi – Norway House Cree Nation (NHCN), Manitoba. He is currently a counsellor at NHCN.

He became a teacher through the Program for the Education of Native Teachers at Brandon University and taught outdoors and math in high school prior to his retirement.

Patricia Holbrow is a River Heights resident and former teacher at Kelvin High School in Winnipeg.

Mabel Horton was born and raised at Nisichawayasihk Cree Nation, where she attended the R.C. Day School, then the Guy Hill and Assiniboia Indian Residential Schools; the latter from the years 1962 to 1967. Mabel was the first registered nurse from her community, having graduated from the Victoria General Hospital in Winnipeg in 1970. Later she obtained her public health nursing diploma, Bachelor of Arts, and a master's degree in Public Administration in 2010. Her places of employment included Winkler Hospital, Norway House Indian Hospital, Cross Lake Nursing Station, God's Lake Narrows and God's River, Eskimo Point (Arviat) Nursing Station, public health, home care, Nisichawayasihk Cree Nation Health and Wellness Centre, Manitoba Keewatin Okimakanak, and the Assembly of Manitoba Chiefs. Since her retirement in 2013, she acts as a (Owecihowew) Knowledge Keeper and advisor for various First Nations health organizations and national and international Indigenous research organizations.

Valerie T. Mainville was born in Fort Frances, Ontario, and raised on the Couchiching First Nation. Her interests in poetry and song began at the age of fifteen, when she began writing poetry and then applied music to the lyrics. In 2008, she self-published two books of poetry, *Poems and Prose on Love and Relationships I* and *II* through Xlibris. These are available on her website, www.poetryofvalerietmainville. com. As a songwriter, she has also self-published two CDs. At present, her works-in-progress include a memoir plus several unpublished scripts and manuscripts. She is enjoying her retirement back in her hometown with family.

Luc Marchildon is the former boys' supervisor and hockey coach at the Assiniboia Indian Residential School. He is originally from Zenon Park in Saskatchewan and was passionate about hockey from a young age, honing his skills with the Oblate fathers who taught at Gravelbourg College in the south of the province. After Assiniboia, he taught at Collège de Saint-Boniface.

As executive director, **Lianna McDonald** leads the Canadian Centre for Child Protection (C3P) in all efforts to reduce the sexual abuse and exploitation of children and assist in the location of missing children. In 1998, Lianna joined the organization—then known as Child Find Manitoba—and guided the agency from a grassroots volunteer organization to a national charity fighting child victimization around the world.

Catherine Mitchell is a policy analyst with the Manitoba Heavy Construction Association and former editorial writer for the *Winnipeg Free Press.*

Mizhakwanigizhik/Nibitaygwanabe (Charlie Nelson) is from Bizhiw Ododaimon (Lynx Clan). He has five children and ten grandchildren. He is a language speaker and Spiritual Leader in Midewiwin. Charlie taught upgrading and basic literacy on seven First Nations (four years), has worked as a drug and alcohol counsellor (twelve years), served as a councillor (eight years), and worked in child and family service and elder support (twenty-five years).

Caroline Perreault (née Seymour) is originally from Hollow Water First Nation. She is a Survivor of two Indian residential schools. She is a retired accountant and has managed her own business. She currently lives in Winnipeg with her husband.

Murray Peterson has been an author and historian for over thirty years. His consultant work has taken him across the country to

242

research train stations, homesteaders, and bush pilots. His work at the City of Winnipeg has given him the opportunity to learn and share the city's colourful history. His wife, four children, and two grandsons are the true joys in his life.

Aila Potosky is a middle-school student who has become deeply interested in humanitarian issues that have occurred in the past and that continue to occur. After learning of the injustices that occurred to Indigenous families, she continues to read and learn of past and present inequalities. She holds hope and optimism, and models acceptance for all races and cultures in hope of a future that embraces diversity.

Gary Robson is a retired educator who, for forty-three years, worked in St. James-Assiniboia School Division as a teacher, counsellor, and administrator. He is a member of the Salvation Army and is very proud of all three of his children.

Betty Ross is originally from Pimicikamak First Nation, known as Cross Lake First Nation, in Treaty 5, Manitoba. She is fluent in her Cree dialect. Betty is a residential school Survivor of two schools, spending more than fifteen years in the system. Today, her pride and joy are her two sons, two daughters, fifteen grandsons, and six great-grand generations. Betty retired from the Winnipeg Regional Health Authority in March 2018, where she worked as a spiritual/cultural care provider. She is currently involved with Seven Oaks School Division as Elder-in-Residence for Elwick School, where she shares her residential school history "Sugar Falls" with kindergarten and grade eight students. Betty's also busy as community Elder, devoting free time with Kairos Blanket Exercises and social justice/climate change issues, and offering Cree classes at the Indigenous Cultural Centre every Wednesday evening. Most recently Betty got involved with Red River College students, sharing her first language, tradi-tional/cultural teachings, drum songs, and so forth. Betty has been gifted as a Knowledge Keeper and Sacred Pipe and Medicine Carrier. She humbly shares these gifts and teachings today and forward throughout the generations. She wants to echo the following Ancient Words of Wisdom: "Always be grateful and thankful for every breath and every step you take on Mother Earth!" Ekosani, Thank you very much.

Carole Starr is from Hollow Water First Nation.

David Montana Wesley is a bookkeeper from Longlac, Ontario.

Andrew Woolford is professor of sociology and criminology at the University of Manitoba, a member of the Royal Society of Canada College, and former president of the International Association of Genocide Scholars. He is author of *This Benevolent Experiment: Indigenous Boarding Schools, Genocide and Redress in the United States and Canada* (2015), *The Politics of Restorative Justice* (2009), and *Between Justice and Certainty: Treaty-Making in British Columbia* (2005), as well as co-author of *Informal Reckonings: Conflict Resolution in Mediation, Restorative Justice, and Reparations* (2005). He is co-editor of *Canada and Colonial Genocide* (2017), *The Idea of a Human Rights Museum* (2015), and *Colonial Genocide in Indigenous North America* (2014).